PHILIP PULLMAN'S

His Dark Materials

Based on the novels by Philip Pullman
Adapted by Nicholas Wright

Heinemann
Inspiring generations

Heinemann Educational Publishers
Halley Court, Jordan Hill, Oxford OX2 8EJ
Part of Harcourt Education

Heinemann is the registered trademark of Harcourt Education Limited

This edition of *His Dark Materials* first published by Heinemann, 2005.
Nicholas Wright's stage adaptation of *His Dark Materials* first published by Nick Hern Books, 2003, and in a revised edition, 2004

2

British Library Cataloguing in Publication Data is available from the British Library on request.

10-digit ISBN: 0 435233 39 4
13-digit ISBN: 978 0 435233 39 6

Typeset by Tek-Art
Original illustrations © Harcourt Education Limited, 2005
Cover design by Forepoint
Printed in the UK by Clays Ltd, St Ives plc

Cover photo: © Jerry Uelsmann (courtesy Laurence Miller Gallery, New York)

Acknowledgements

Every effort has been made to contact copyright holders of material reproduced in this book. Any omissions will be rectified in subsequent printings if notice is given to the publishers.

The publishers would like to thank the following for permission to reproduce photographs

p145–7, 283, Catherine Ashmore

Contents

Scheme of work and teaching resources
To help deliver the activities on pages 283–314, extensive teaching materials are available to download free from www.heinemann.co.uk/literature

Introduction by Philip Pullman

The very first thought I had about *His Dark Materials* was an image of a small girl going into a room she shouldn't have entered, having to hide when someone came in and then overhearing something she shouldn't have known about.

It all grew out of that. It was very important that any adaptation should put this little girl, whom I later came to know as Lyra, right at the heart of the story. *His Dark Materials* takes up three books (*Northern Lights*, *The Subtle Knife* and *The Amber Spyglass*) and 1300 pages. How could it ever be made to work on the stage? Well, the answer, as Nicholas Wright discovered when he wrote this brilliant adaptation, is to keep Lyra and her quest in mind from the very beginning. Everything else – the daemons, the huge conflicts, the strange adventures in stranger worlds – all falls into place once that central truth is understood.

The opening Nicholas Wright found is one of the cleverest strokes of stagecraft I've ever seen. It explains so many things at once: what daemons are; who Lyra and Will are and why children can be played by adults (because both plays are one long flashback, in effect); and it gives us something to remember and be enlightened by at the very end, when we see the two of them again on the bench under the tree.

Actually, in one way the plays are better than the novels. In the book I had Lyra and Will arranging to 'meet' in the Botanic Gardens, in their separate worlds, every midsummer's day at noon. How much better it is for them to meet at midnight, as Nicholas Wright has it. I wish I'd thought of that.

So here is another way of telling the story of Lyra and Will. It's not better, it's not worse; this way works on the stage, and my way works on the page. I hope you enjoy reading it, and perhaps acting in it, as much as I enjoyed watching it all come into being.

Philip Pullman

Introduction by Nicholas Wright

When I first read *His Dark Materials* I didn't know that I would be asked to adapt it. I simply read it as every reader does, whatever age, racing from world to world from the first mysterious moments in the Retiring Room to the heart-breaking – yet optimistic – ending.

To turn the three books (*Northern Lights*, *The Subtle Knife* and *The Amber Spyglass)* all by Philip Pullman into two plays was one of the most difficult things I've ever done. I had to change some of the story, cut some characters and invent one of my own. My aim, always, was not just to write a cut-down reproduction of these books but to create the template for a thrilling piece of theatre that captured their spirit. I was encouraged in all this by Nicholas Hytner, who directed the plays at the National Theatre in London, and by Philip Pullman himself, who was always the first to say, 'Don't worry. The books are one thing, and the plays are another.'

The National Theatre gave these plays a tremendous production. The daemons were lively puppets lit up from within, the stage-machinery brought the scenery up from beneath the stage and down from above, while a huge mirror extended the Land of the Dead into eternity. No other theatre in Britain, or perhaps anywhere in the world, could stage them so elaborately.

But I've always thought that if they can't be done in a spectacular way, like the National Theatre did, then the other best approach is to do them very simply, using the power of the imagination. Go back to the books, be inspired by what you find there about the daemons, the flying witches, the tiny Gallivespians, the battles, the windows, the Aurora and everything else, and then invent your own way of showing them. The important thing is that the action never stops!

Nicholas Wright

Cast List

Part 1

Lyra Belacqua
Pantalaimon, *her deamon*
Will Parry

OXFORD
Master of Jordan College
Professor Hopcraft
Professor Tonkin

Lord Asriel
Stelmaria, *his daemon*
Thorold, *his manservant*

Mrs Coulter
The Golden Monkey, *her daemon*

Fra Pavel, *an emissary from Geneva*

Cawson, *Steward of Jordan College*
Mrs Lonsdale, *Housekeeper*
Roger Parslow, *a kitchen boy*
Salcilia, *his daemon*
Billy Costa
Tony Costa

LONDON
Lord Boreal

Daisy
Jessie
Lily

Stallholder
Top-hatted man
Ben, *Tony Costa's friend*

TROLLESUND
John Faa, *Lord of the Western gyptians*
Farder Coram

Iorek Byrnison, *an armoured bear*
Bear-keeper
Mayor

Kaisa, *Serafina's daemon*
Lee Scoresby, *a balloonist*
Hester, *his daemon*

BOLVANGAR
Sister Clara
Sister Betty
Dr West
Dr Cade
Dr Sargent
Tortured witch

SVALBARD
Ifor Raknison, *King of armoured bears*
Bear Patrol

GENEVA
President of the Consistorial Court
Brother Jasper
Perpetua, *his daemon*

LAPLAND
Serafina Pekkala, *Queen of the Lapland witches*

Ruta Skadi, *Queen of the Latvian witches*
Pipistrelle
Caitlin
Grimhild
Grendella

Jopari, *a Shaman*

CITAGAZZE
Angelica
Paolo
Giacomo Paradisi
Tullio

OXFORD
Librarian
Assistant

Part 1

Act One

Scene 1

Oxford/Oxford. ***The Botanic Gardens****. Night. A tree with spreading branches. Lyra and Will, both aged about twenty, are waiting on a wooden bench. Will has an old green leather writing case.*

A clock strikes twelve.

LYRA Will?

WILL Lyra?

LYRA This morning I half woke up, and I felt so happy. Even before I knew what day it was. Then I remembered it was Midsummer Day. I looked at the clock and I thought, it's only sixteen hours to midnight. Sixteen hours, and I'll be sitting right next to you.

WILL I had to scramble over the wall this time. There was a copper on duty till quarter to twelve.

LYRA I know you're there.

Pause.

WILL I'm wearing my one good shirt and I've cleaned my trainers. I don't usually look so smart. I'm sharing a house now with three other students, and one of them said, 'Hello, Will, don't tell us you've got a date at last.' I said, I do, in fact. He said, 'Oh, nice one, when do we get to meet her?' I said, that might be difficult.

He laughs, then stops.

I still miss you.

PANTALAIMON Say something.

LYRA I will when I'm ready, Pan.

WILL I miss Pantalaimon too. Your daemon. Your soul. I miss him as much as I miss you. Because he *is* you.

PANTALAIMON Tell him about the college.

WILL I know he's there. I know *you're* there. Even though you're further away from me than the furthest star … you're here. Right here. On the same bench. In a different world.

LYRA I've had a very good year at college. It's like they told me, all those years ago … if I work very hard I can start, just start to do the things that came so naturally to me when I was a kid.

WILL 'I spread my wings, and I brush ten million other worlds, and they know nothing of it.'

LYRA It's different for me, from what it's like for the other students. Jordan College is new for them. They see the obvious things, like books and towers and ancient stones. I see the place where I grew up. I see Mrs Lonsdale, who was meant to look after me and keep me tidy …

Mrs Lonsdale is there to change Lyra's clothes.

MRS LONSDALE Just what did you think you were wearing, Miss Lyra?

LYRA I see the mouseholes and the secret doorways, and the hiding-places. And the mouldy old scholars with their flapping gowns. I see Roger, like he was on the day I met him. I was twelve. Me and the other college kids had been fighting the kids from town. Then we all joined up to fight the brick-burners' kids down by the clay-pits. And then we remembered it was the horse-fair week … so we all rushed down to the river to fight the gyptian kids. I was fighting Billy Costa.

Scene 2

Lyra's Oxford. *Will and his world disappear. Lyra is twelve. Assorted kids are yelling at the gyptian kids:*

Oi! Gyppoes!
Water rats!
Fortune-tellers!
Tea-leaves!
Want any knives sharpened?
Any old iron!

Gyptian kids and other kids fight. Lyra gets Billy Costa down on the ground in a headlock. The others clear.

LYRA Give up, Billy?

BILLY No!

LYRA Now?

BILLY No!

LYRA What about now?

BILLY Yeah! Get off.

They stand.

How'd you do that?

LYRA It's a headlock. Look, I'll show you.

BILLY Leave off!

Billy's brother Tony appears.

TONY Oi, Billy! Our ma says, get back home this minute or she'll give you a clip.

LYRA Hello, Tony.

TONY Don't you 'hello' me, you horrible little tyke. Wasn't it you throwing mud at our boat just now?

LYRA That weren't me. It was some other kids.

TONY Oh yeah!

LYRA They come down from Abingdon in a special coach … all painted black, with a skeleton driving. And he saw your boat, and he pointed his bony finger …

TONY Oh aye. Lyra the liar. En't that what they call you? Go on, get back home. Come on, Billy.

He and Billy go. Lyra stays, dejected. Roger runs on.

ROGER Where's the fighting?

LYRA You missed it.

ROGER Who won?

LYRA Dunno. Don't matter either. See yer, whoever you are.

ROGER See yer.

They turn to go.

PANTALAIMON I'm Pantalaimon.

SALCILIA I'm Salcilia.

PANTALAIMON I en't seen you before.

SALCILIA That's 'cause we only just arrived from London.

The daemons approach each other. Lyra and Roger look at them in surprise.

ROGER That's funny.

LYRA They wanna be friends.

ROGER That could be. My mum always says, you know at once when you like somebody. An' I like you. I'm Roger. Roger Parslow. My dad's the new head gardener at Gabriel College, an' me mum's a cook an' I'm gonna be a kitchen-boy.

LYRA I'm Lyra Belacqua an' I'm at Jordan College. I don't work there or nothing. I just play around.

ROGER Jordan's bigger'n Gabriel, en't it?

LYRA It's bigger an' richer an' ever so much more important. You wanna see it?

ROGER Yeah, don't mind.

LYRA Come on then.

They walk on.

ROGER Where's *your* mum an' dad?

LYRA En't got none. I'm nearly an orphan.

ROGER You can't be *nearly* an orphan.

LYRA You can if you're me. I got an uncle, and he's famous.

ROGER Bet I never heard of 'im.

LYRA Bet you have.

ROGER So what's his name?

LYRA Lord Asriel.

ROGER *Him?* What, the explorer an' all?

LYRA That's right.

ROGER Well that *is* famous. What's he like?

LYRA He's old, like … forty at least. And he's *ferocious*. There was some Tartars caught him once, and they tied him up, and one of 'em was gonna cut his guts out, and Lord Asriel looked at him – just looked, like that – and he dropped down dead.

PANTALAIMON Lyra the liar!

LYRA It was summat like that.

They have arrived at Jordan College. Scholars are circulating. A couple of students cycle past. The Master appears with Fra Pavel.

Right, this is the quad, an' underneath us there's the crypt, with tunnels windin' everywhere like a 'normous sponge. An' those are the scholars, an' that's the Master of the College.

ROGER Who's that snakey feller who's picking his nose?

LYRA That's Fra Pavel. He comes to look at me twice a year and asks me questions.

MASTER Lyra, one moment.

Lyra approaches.

Fra Pavel is here. He arrived this morning from the Consistorial Court of Discipline in Geneva to inspect your progress.

FRA PAVEL Good evening, Lyra.

LYRA *(guarded)* 'ello.

FRA PAVEL Are you still happy at Jordan College?

LYRA Sort of.

FRA PAVEL Do you learn your lessons? Do you say your prayers to the Authority?

LYRA Mm hm.

FRA PAVEL Have you decided what you will do, once you've grown up and your daemon is settled?

LYRA I'll go exploring with Lord Asriel. He's gonna take me up the Amazon river, or into the desert, or the Arctic Circle …

FRA PAVEL Is this true?

MASTER No, not at all. You surely remember her weakness for fantastic stories. Your uncle is far too busy to see you when he comes to Jordan College, isn't he, Lyra?

LYRA But he's coming on Wednesday week. Mrs Lonsdale told me. And he'll see me then, I'm gonna make sure he does. I'll follow him round, till …

FRA PAVEL *(to Lyra)* Play with your friend.

Lyra goes.

Why was I not informed of Lord Asriel's visit?

MASTER I would have warned you, if you'd given me time. Lord Asriel has offered to show us the findings of his latest expedition to the Arctic. Some of the scholars are most enthusiastic. Others, of course, are as shocked as you. I try to steer a moderate course, but …

FRA PAVEL There *is* no moderate course. You are either for the Church or you're against it. Don't you *see* that? Don't you know what's happening outside your smug little ivory tower? Fears of war. Rebellion. Dissent, confusion, schism, doubt. All fuelled by the mad ambitions of Lord Asriel and the complacency of academics like yourself.

MASTER Then what must I do?

FRA PAVEL Since that heretic has been foolish enough to place himself in your hands, you must take advantage of it. You must render him harmless, by the most extreme of measures. Is that agreed?

MASTER No, certainly not! Or only if … though, on the other hand … I'll do as you say. But under protest.

FRA PAVEL Let's walk on.

They do.

Lyra has changed. I see in her, both the child she is, and the woman she will become.

MASTER Is anything wrong with that?

FRA PAVEL Time will tell.

They go.

Scene 3

Two weeks later. ***Oxford.*** *Evening. Scholars appear, and continue to assemble. Lyra and Roger enter.*

LYRA He's here, Pan. He's here!

1ST SCHOLAR *(to Lyra)* Out of the Quad! Out of the Quad! He's here! Look, there's his zeppelin!

They look.

2ND SCHOLAR I do believe he's mooring it to the roof of the chapel.

3RD SCHOLAR Disgraceful.

5TH SCHOLAR Rather amusing, though!

4TH SCHOLAR *(who is very old)* Is something happening?

1ST SCHOLAR Yes, Lord Asriel's just arrived.

4TH SCHOLAR What did he say?

Someone explains silently, as:

1ST SCHOLAR We'll exchange a few polite formalities, and then we'll take him through to dinner in the Great Hall.

2ND SCHOLAR Look! He's getting out!

The 6th Scholar – Professor Hopcraft – has arrived.

HOPCRAFT Gentlemen, gentlemen! What's going on? It's not a *welcoming* party, surely?

3RD SCHOLAR We mustn't let Lord Asriel think that we approve of him.

1ST SCHOLAR Well, some of us do.

Disagreement breaks out, as:

5TH SCHOLAR The Master's gone to greet him, so he can't be totally in disgrace.

Thorold appears, followed by a college servant, Cawson, who is carrying equipment.

2ND SCHOLAR There's his manservant.

SEVERAL Welcome, Thorold!

THOROLD Evening, gentlemen.

1ST SCHOLAR The lecture is in the Retiring Room, just behind the Lodge.

THOROLD I en't forgotten my way, sir. Mind that box, Mr Cawson, there's glass inside it.

He goes.

1ST SCHOLAR I hear that Lord Asriel is going to give us a magic-lantern show.

HOPCRAFT Is he? Really? Doesn't that smack of entertainment?

The Master appears.

MASTER Our guest is here.

Lord Asriel enters with his snow-leopard daemon, Stelmaria. There's a ripple of applause from the scholars, who shake his hand while greetings are exchanged. Lyra tries hard to attract his attention.

LORD ASRIEL *(to a scholar)* Professor Tonkin, I hear your book's been a great success.

LYRA Hello!

Lord Asriel ignores her, and the Master bustles her aside.

MASTER Out of the way!

LORD ASRIEL *(to another)* Congratulations on your professorship, Richard.

Lyra is back.

LYRA It's me!

MASTER Now then, Lyra!

She is shunted out of the way.

LORD ASRIEL Professor Hopcraft, may I say how much I admire your writing?

HOPCRAFT *(charmed)* Oh, you've read it? Well I'm flattered. Though I …

MASTER Shall we go to the dining hall, my lord?

Lyra and Roger watch as they all go.

ROGER He's awesome.

She starts to go.

Hey, where you goin'?

LYRA Where d'you think? We're gonna sneak into the Retiring Room while they're still having their dinner. I know a secret way.

PANTALAIMON Lyra, we can't! It en't just any old room.

SALCILIA Kids can't go in there, and nor can women.

PANTALAIMON Yeah, and it's probably haunted.

LYRA Good, that settles it. Come on Rodge, this is gonna be fun.

Scene 4

They go. ***The Retiring Room*** *appears. Thorold and Cawson are there, Cawson setting down a tray with a glass and a decanter.*

CAWSON This wine is for Lord Asriel's pleasure only. It's the 1898.

THOROLD That's very thoughtful of the Master. It's his lordship's favourite year. After you, Mr Cawson.

They go. Lyra and Roger appear through a secret doorway. They look round.

LYRA Wow.

ROGER It's spooky all right.

PANTALAIMON This is a bad idea.

Roger finds the projector.

ROGER 'Ere, look.

SALCILIA Don't touch it!

ROGER I won't break it.

He looks.

'Ere, Lyra, come an' look. This is fancy.

Lyra is looking at the walls.

LYRA I wanna look at them paintings. All the Masters with their daemons.

PANTALAIMON Now that *is* interesting.

LYRA He's got a falcon daemon.

PANTALAIMON He's got a magpie.

LYRA That one's got an owl. He must have been specially clever.

A bell is heard.

They've finished dinner! Let's go back in here. Pan, Salcilia, change into something small.

The daemons change into moths. Lyra and Roger hide. The Master comes in. He looks round and, having established that the room is empty, takes a small phial from his pocket, empties it into the decanter and creeps out. Lyra and Roger appear.

LYRA He poisoned the wine!

ROGER How d'you know it's poison?

LYRA It must be. Why else did he look around like that, all furtive-like?

PANTALAIMON You can't jump out and make a fuss, we'll get into trouble.

LYRA I can't let Lord Asriel be murdered, Pan!

ROGER Shuddup! He's here!

Lord Asriel comes in with Stelmaria and Thorold, who adjusts the projection equipment. Lyra and Roger get out of sight. Pantalaimon and Salcilia watch.

LORD ASRIEL Is everything set up?

THOROLD It is, sir.

LORD ASRIEL Excellent. The sooner I can get out of this place, the better.

Cawson comes in with a cup of coffee on a tray.

CAWSON Good evening, my lord.

LORD ASRIEL Good evening, Cawson. Is that the College Tokay I can see on the table?

CAWSON It is, sir. There are only three bottles left in the cellars. The Keeper of Wine was somewhat taken aback, but the Master was most particular.

THOROLD Thank you, Mr Cawson.

Cawson and Thorold go. Lord Asriel goes to pour wine. Lyra watches in great suspense.

LORD ASRIEL Smell the air. Must, fust and dry bones. Nothing has changed. Nothing is new. I'd like to smash those windows and let some air in.

STELMARIA You're tired. You ought to be resting.

LORD ASRIEL I know, I know. And I ought to have changed my clothes. There's probably some ancient etiquette that allows them to fine me half a swan and a bottle of claret for being improperly dressed.

He is about to drink.

LYRA No!

LORD ASRIEL Who's there?

LYRA Don't drink it!

She scrambles forward to snatch the glass from his hand.

LORD ASRIEL Lyra! What are you doing in here?

LYRA Throw it away! It's poisoned.

LORD ASRIEL What did you say?

LYRA I saw the Master pouring something into it.

LORD ASRIEL The *Master*?

LYRA Yeah. I was hiding in there, an' …

Lord Asriel sees Roger.

LORD ASRIEL Who's that?

LYRA That's Roger. He's my best friend. 'Ere, Rodge …!

LORD ASRIEL Stay where you are, young man. One bothersome child is quite enough. *(to Lyra)* Why were you hiding?

LYRA I wanted to see you. I wanted to ask you when you'd take me to the Arctic, so I'd …

LORD ASRIEL Don't be ridiculous. You're a child.

LYRA But …

LORD ASRIEL Don't argue with me. I have to get back to the Arctic and I don't have any money. That's why I'm here. I'm trying to get the college to pay for the expedition, and they don't know that yet. Go away. No, stop. Let me look at you.

He looks at her.

You seem healthy enough. Show me your hands.

She does.

Disgusting. Where do you play, to get so dirty?

LYRA In the claypits. An' up on the roofs. Rodge an' me found a rook up there. It'd hurt its foot. I was gonna cook it an' eat it, but Rodge said we oughta make it better, so we gave it some wine and some bits of food, an' …

THOROLD The scholars are here, my lord.

LORD ASRIEL Here are five gold dollars for you. Get back where you were. Go on!

Lyra hides. The Master comes in, followed by scholars, and is astonished to see Lord Asriel standing with the decanter in his hand.

MASTER Lord Asriel!

LORD ASRIEL Wrong vintage, Master. Thorold, would you mind turning down the lamps?

Thorold does and the Scholars take their seats. Lord Asriel begins.

LORD ASRIEL Before I show you what I found in the Arctic, I'm going to explain to you why I went there. I was a student here at Jordan College. Some of you taught me. I was young, I was rebellious, and I longed with all my heart to find the answers to those questions that have baffled experimental theologians for centuries. And I still do. Let's start with daemons. Each of us has one.

There's a nonplussed reaction from the humans, but the daemons show great interest.

We can't imagine a world without them. But what do we really know about our daemons? What do they know about us?

STELMARIA No more than you.

LORD ASRIEL Exactly. Isn't it time that we knew … let's say … why they reflect our natures in the way they do? Why is Stelmaria a snow-leopard while the Master's daemon is a raven? Why are our daemons fixed in one particular shape? Why can't they change?

3RD SCHOLAR *(stating the obvious)* Because we're adults!

LORD ASRIEL Yet a child's daemon can change whenever it wants to. Why's that? Why can't we touch each others' daemons? Why, if some lunatic were to pull Stelmaria and me apart, would both she and I suffer such agony? And why, if we were separated, would we die? I've done years of research and experiment on this very question, and it seems to me now that the answer lies in that mysterious substance … or power … or essence … that all of us know about, and that none of us truly understands. I mean the elementary particles that we call … Dust.

Hopcraft springs up.

HOPCRAFT I understood that talk about Dust was not allowed. What is Fra Pavel's view?

MASTER Fra Pavel is in Geneva. But he told me before he left, that we should watch our tongues.

HOPCRAFT Then we could all be in very deep water indeed …

Lord Asriel overrides him.

LORD ASRIEL *This*, gentlemen, is why I went to the Arctic. To find the man who knows more about Dust than anyone else alive: a certain spirit-diviner, an occultist, a *shaman* as he's known to the Northern tribesmen. His name is Jopari. This is a photogram that I took of him on the day we met.

A slide comes up of Jopari standing in the moonlight in the snow, beside a hut, with one hand raised.

There he stands, one hand raised up in greeting. The photogram I shall show you next was taken from the same position a moment later, by a secret process that Jopari taught me. It uses instead of the normal emulsion, an amber liquid that reveals those things that cannot be seen by the naked eye.

A slide comes up of the same scene, but with a fountain of sparks streaming from Jopari's raised hand. The Scholars gasp in astonishment.

Dust is bathing him in radiance. Just as it does to all of us, every moment of our adult lives. But with us, that radiance is invisible. Here, for the first time in human history, we can see it. Here at last we have a clue to the nature of Dust. Where does it come from? The picture seems to show it streaming down from the sky. Is that the answer? But why has it collected around the spirit-diviner in such vast quantity? Has it *recognised* his special gifts? Has Dust an intelligence?

Animated conversation breaks out between the Scholars.

MASTER Gentlemen, please!

LORD ASRIEL And it was this, that led me to the most extraordinary discovery of all. Here is a photogram of the Aurora Borealis, which I took in the old-fashioned way.

A slide comes up of the Aurora Borealis.

4TH SCHOLAR Forgive my ignorance, but if I ever knew what the Aurora was, I have forgotten. Is it the Northern Lights?

LORD ASRIEL It is. But by using Jopari's secret process, I revealed something I could hardly believe myself.

A second slide appears, looking much the same as the previous one.

3RD SCHOLAR It's just the same.

1ST SCHOLAR No … there's something different in the centre.

2ND SCHOLAR Lord Asriel, could you enlarge it, please?

Lord Asriel does. A city appears in the Aurora.

LORD ASRIEL We see a … city! Towers, domes, walls, buildings, streets, even a line of palm trees … suspended in the air … all clearly visible through the boundaries of the world we know.

5TH SCHOLAR Are you saying this city is outside our world?

LORD ASRIEL It's in a *different* world! Think what that means. If Dust can travel from world to world, then so can light. If light can travel, then so can we. The doors are open to us. The chains are broken. We can question everything we've been taught. We can challenge every dreary, grey belief that we've had dinned into our skulls. Our reach is infinite, and I shall prove it. I shall go back to the Arctic. I'll find the Aurora. I'll build a pathway through its heart into this different world, and I'll cross into it! Will this college support me?

HOPCRAFT Certainly not. This is blatant support for a highly dangerous theory!

OTHERS Name it!/What theory?

HOPCRAFT I mean the multi-world theory as you, Professor Chalker, very well know …

1ST SCHOLAR I propose that we grant Lord Asriel a handsome subvention from the college funds.

SCHOLARS Hear hear!

The Master springs up.

MASTER Lord Asriel, you have gone too far!

LORD ASRIEL Put it to the vote.

6TH SCHOLAR All in favour?

Most scholars raise their hands.

3RD SCHOLAR Those against?

A few scholars raise their hands.

MASTER The motion is carried.

The meeting breaks up in pandemonium.

3RD SCHOLAR Dust is evil! Dust is the mark of sin!

ANTI The Church has put three centuries of thought into this very question, and I really do think that we have to accept its judgement./We ought to be fighting Dust, not talking about it./Lord Asriel has been a menace to Jordan College ever since I knew him as an undergraduate./The Church will make a stink and close down our research programmes./Who says those photograms are real? They don't look real to me. They could all be a fake. (etc.)

PRO I've known for *years* and *years* that the multi-world theory is solid fact but .../Well the camera doesn't lie. It doesn't. Really it doesn't. I mean, we've seen the palm trees and the city and all the rest of it .../My students think I'm a boring old fossil because I cannot admit the truth./*What* did you say? *What did* you say? (etc.)

Scene 5

Six weeks later. Jordan College. Day, outside. Lyra, Roger, Pantalaimon and Salcilia. Lyra is downcast.

ROGER Cheer up.

LYRA I can't. It's six weeks gone since Lord Asriel went to the Arctic, an' he en't never wrote nor nothing.

ROGER I thought you said he never does.

LYRA But it's different this time, en't it? I saved his life. You'd think a postcard wouldn't be too much bother.

PANTALAIMON Or a carrier-pigeon.

ROGER It were something though, weren't it? All them scholars standing on chairs an' shoutin' ...

LYRA ... and the man with his hand held up. You know what, Rodge?

ROGER No, what?

LYRA If I go to the Arctic … *when* I go … I'm gonna take you with me.

ROGER I never thought no different.

Mrs Lonsdale appears.

MRS LONSDALE There you are. Lyra, you're to come with me and visit the Master. No time to wash, we'll have to make do with hankie and spit.

She does.

LYRA I don't wanna see him!

ROGER He's a poisoner!

MRS LONSDALE What are you talking about, you two? He's a lovely, kind old gentleman who wouldn't say boo to a goose. There, that's better.

They walk on.

And never again let me find you out and about without no grown-ups.

LYRA Why not?

MRS LONSDALE Why not? 'Cause it's not safe any more, that's why. There's kids being stolen away in broad daylight, not that anyone knows who's taking 'em.

LYRA It's the Gobblers take 'em.

MRS LONSDALE Yes, but who's the Gobblers? That's the question.

ROGER My dad says there en't no Gobblers. He says it's all got up by the papers.

MRS LONSDALE Well he's wrong, quite wrong. There's Gobblers all over the country.

LYRA But there en't none in Oxford, is there, Mrs Lonsdale?

MRS LONSDALE I'm afraid there is. I didn't want to upset you, but you'll hear about it soon enough. Young Billy Costa's gone.

LYRA What, Billy, my mate?

ROGER How did it happen?

MRS LONSDALE It was just like *that*. He was holding a horse for his brother Tony, and Tony took his eye off him just for a minute, and when he looked back, Billy had vanished.

LYRA Isn't nobody gonna look for him?

MRS LONSDALE The gyptians will, 'cause they look after their own. But us landlopers won't be bothering, sad to say. Here we are.

They have arrived at the Master's study.

ROGER Don't drink nothing he gives you.

LYRA Yeah, and you wait outside and listen, and if I scream for help, you gotta come running in.

The Master's Study. *Mrs Lonsdale knocks on the door.*

MASTER Come.

Lyra and Mrs Lonsdale go in. The Master is there.

MRS LONSDALE No one keeping an eye on her, Master, and the Gobblers in Oxford too.

MASTER Thank you, Mrs Lonsdale.

She goes.

Sit down, Lyra.

Lyra does.

You have been in the care of Jordan College for twelve years now, ever since you were brought here as a baby. We are fond of you, you've never been a bad child and you've been happy, I think, in your own way. But that part of your life has ended.

LYRA What do you mean?

MASTER A very well-known and distinguished person has offered to take you away.

LYRA You mean Lord Asriel?

MASTER No! Lord Asriel cannot communicate with anyone.

LYRA Is he dead?

MASTER No, certainly not. He went to the Arctic, as you know, and I have reason to believe he's safe. Now, as for you. There is a friend of the college, a wealthy widow, who has offered to take you to live with her in London.

LYRA I don't want no bloody widow! I wanna stay here!

MASTER Lyra …

Mrs Coulter appears: a beautiful woman wearing a long yellow-red fox-fur coat. Her daemon is a golden monkey.

MRS COULTER May I speak to her?

MASTER Certainly, Mrs Coulter. This is Lyra.

Mrs Coulter looks at her.

LYRA What you lookin' at?

MRS COULTER You. I haven't seen you since … well, ever. And you're just as they described you. Do you like chocolatl? I think I have some in my bag.

Lyra receives the chocolatl with a show of indifference.

I know how nervous you must be feeling. I'm a little nervous myself, believe it or not. It's just so … very strange to meet you. But we'll take it gently, just to begin with. And we'll soon be friends.

LYRA I've got a friend. I play with him all the time.

Mrs Coulter turns questioningly to the Master.

MASTER He's a college serving boy. His name is Roger.

MRS COULTER A college servant? Well, I mustn't interfere. I'm sure that whatever I say to her, she'll do the opposite.

LYRA Yes I will.

Mrs Coulter laughs. To Lyra:

MRS COULTER That is *exactly* what I would have said myself, at your age. But seriously, Lyra, don't you think you're getting a little too grown up for rough-and-tumble games with boys from a different background? You'll be a young woman soon, and … let me look at you properly … yes, you could be a very pretty one. Wouldn't you like that?

LYRA What, just being pretty all day?

MRS COULTER Oh, more than that. You'll be my personal assistant.

MASTER Mrs Coulter is the Chief Executive Officer of a very significant organisation.

LYRA What's it called?

MRS COULTER It's called the General Oblation Board.

LYRA What's an Obla … Oblacious?

MASTER The word 'oblate', Lyra, dates from the Middle Ages, when parents would present their children to the Church to be monks or nuns. It means a sacrifice, a giving-away of something precious …

Mrs Coulter silences him with a look.

MRS COULTER Let's not confuse her, Master. *(to Lyra)* All that you need to know for now, is that the General Oblation Board is a charitable research foundation that finds out all about Dust. Have you heard about Dust?

LYRA I have, yeah … but I thought we wasn't supposed to talk about it.

MRS COULTER You can if you have permission. And the Church has given the General Oblation Board its total backing. I shall want you to meet my clients, keep my appointment book … you'd like that, wouldn't you?

It's clear that Lyra wouldn't.

There'll be my travel arrangements too, of course. I travel a great deal.

LYRA Where to?

MRS COULTER The Arctic, mostly. I have some very interesting projects in that part of the world.

LYRA Would I come with you?

MRS COULTER Do you want to?

Lyra disguises her eagerness.

LYRA I didn't say that. I'm just asking.

Mrs Coulter changes tack.

MRS COULTER Well, one could *make* it a part of your job, I suppose … but I wonder how much you'd really enjoy it … flying in a zeppelin … watching the icebergs floating past us, miles below … wouldn't it be too adventurous for you?

LYRA No, but … No, it wouldn't.

MRS COULTER And once we get there, there'll be lots of dreadfully dangerous creatures … witches, hungry cliff-ghasts. Armoured bears … the bravest fighters on earth, but oh, so frightening … you wouldn't like meeting one of *them*, I'm sure.

LYRA I might not mind.

MRS COULTER But now I think of it … isn't there someone very special in the Arctic? Someone you'd like to see, who I could take you to?

LYRA Do you know Lord Asriel?

MRS COULTER I know him *very* well. So … will you come to London?

Lyra hesitates.

MASTER The truth is, Lyra, that neither you nor I can choose where we wish to go. We are moved by tides much fiercer than you can imagine, and they sweep us all into the current.

MRS COULTER Thank you, Master, you've been extremely helpful. I shall inform Geneva. Good night, Lyra. We'll leave in the morning.

LYRA In the morning?

Mrs Coulter hugs her.

MRS COULTER Dear child! We're going to have such fun! *(to the Master)* Good night.

She goes. Lyra is about to follow her.

MASTER One moment, Lyra. Were you by any chance concealed in the Retiring Room, the night Lord Asriel spoke to the Scholars?

LYRA I might have been.

MASTER So you have reason to mistrust me.

LYRA Yeah, I do.

MASTER You must understand, a man in my position has to commit some harm from time to time, in order to prevent some greater evil. But one can try to make up for it. There will be dangers where you are going. You will need protection. I am giving you this.

He produces a small package wrapped in black velvet, and unwraps it to reveal a gold compass-like object.

LYRA What is it?

MASTER It is an alethiometer. It was constructed in Prague three hundred years ago. Only six were ever made, and even fewer survive. Lord Asriel presented this one to the college when he was young.

LYRA What does it do?

MASTER It tells the truth. But it does so in a way so deep and so mysterious that adults need a whole library of reference books to understand it.

LYRA What about children?

MASTER Who can say? Innocence can be wiser than experience. If you could read it, Lyra, even if only a very little, it would be the greatest treasure you ever possessed. Respect it. Keep it safe. Tell no one you have it.

LYRA Not even Mrs Coulter?

MASTER *(emphatically)* Not even her. Now take it and go.

Lyra takes the alethiometer and goes into the night outside.

LYRA Roger! Roger!

Mrs Lonsdale appears, carrying a lantern.

Oh, Mrs Lonsdale. Have you seen Roger?

MRS LONSDALE No, I haven't. Nobody has. They can't find him anywhere.

LYRA What?

MRS LONSDALE He was standing here. Right here. I told him he ought to go home. And now the Gobblers have taken him. Oh, that stupid, stupid boy!

LYRA How can you say that? Don't you care about Roger?

MRS LONSDALE People care about things in different ways, Miss Lyra. We don't all show it. Roger's my nephew.

LYRA I didn't know.

MRS LONSDALE You didn't know because you never asked. He was waiting for *you*.

She moves away, peering into the darkness.

LYRA He's gone.

PANTALAIMON Salcilia too.

LYRA Can you feel it, Pan? It's like I'm only half of meself, and the other half's just … not there.

PANTALAIMON You still got me.

LYRA Yeah.

She hugs Pantalaimon.

I'd die if I didn't. And you know what, Pan? Whatever they've done to Roger, wherever they've taken him … we're gonna find him. We're gonna rescue him. I swear it.

Scene 6

A bleak collection point. *A brazier is burning. Children are waiting, with suitcases by their sides. They have all just finished writing letters. Among them are Daisy, Jessie and Lily. Billy Costa is there. An old servant hands round mugs of hot chocolatl. Roger appears.*

ROGER 'ello.

SEVERAL 'ello.

BILLY Rodge! 'ello!

ROGER 'ello, Billy.

BILLY Come an' sit down. *(to the child beside him)* Move up, willya?

He catches the servant's eye and points to Roger.

Oi, Miss. Don't forget the new boy.

Roger sits by him. The servant gives Roger a mugful of chocolatl. Meanwhile:

'ere, Ratter. You know Roger. Say 'ello.

Ratter, his daemon, turns away.

Nah, she's gloomy today.

ROGER Billy …

BILLY Yeah?

ROGER … 'ave we been taken by the Gobblers?

BILLY Sure 'ave, mate.

ROGER What they gonna do to us?

BILLY Nothin' nasty.

The other children chip in, trying to keep up their spirits.

DAISY We all gotta write letters to our mums and dads. In case they're worried about us, know what I mean?

JESSIE Catch mine getting worried.

ROGER Is it all right, then? Being a Gobbler victim?

DAISY Yeah, it's nice.

JESSIE We're gettin' to like it, en't we, Lily?

LILY We're goin' on a boat.

ROGER A *boat*? Where to?

LILY Dunno, but it's gotta be more excitin' than being at 'ome.

JESSIE I hope it's somewhere 'ot.

LILY Yeah, with long white beaches.

JESSIE Or a swimmin' pool!

They all laugh.

DAISY Ssh! Look be'ind you.

She indicates the tail of the golden monkey, which has appeared somewhere. Mrs Coulter appears.

MRS COULTER Have you finished your letters, children?

ALL Yes, miss.

MRS COULTER Hold them out.

They do, and she collects them.

MRS COULTER Have you all been given a suitcase?

ALL Yes, miss.

MRS COULTER And your pyjamas? Nighties? Toothbrushes?

ALL Yes, miss!

MRS COULTER And who likes chocolatl?

ALL Me! Me!

MRS COULTER Well, I happen to know that they'll be handing some out to you the minute you get on board.

ALL Hooray!

The golden monkey attracts Mrs Coulter's attention.

MRS COULTER What?

He points out Roger.

ROGER Who, me?

MRS COULTER Oh dear, you didn't have time to write. But I can give your mother a message.

ROGER Will you tell her …

MRS COULTER Yes?

ROGER … to feed my budgie?

MRS COULTER Isn't there something more important?

ROGER Just say I love her.

MRS COULTER She'll be so happy to hear that!

A ship's hooter blows. A door opens and a sea captain appears. The children file out.

Form a line … that's right … There'll be a nurse to look after you … make sure you tell her if you're feeling sea-sick … Ladies first, Billy … No pushing each other on the gang-plank. Goodbye!

The last children to leave wave and call 'Goodbye!' Mrs Coulter gives the letters to the golden monkey and leaves. He burns the letters.

Scene 7

Mrs Coulter's living room. *Lyra, prettily dressed, is admiring herself in a mirror. To Pantalaimon:*

LYRA I en't never been pretty before. Never in all my life. I en't never had my hair done proper, and my nails all pink and polished.

PANTALAIMON She's just turning you into a pet.

LYRA She loves me, though, I'm sure she does. She sits on the end of my bed when she thinks I'm asleep, and she looks at me, so sad, with those big dark eyes.

PANTALAIMON If she's so good, then why's she got such a horrible, evil daemon?

LYRA I dunno. But I know what you mean. It's like she's evil and good all at the same time.

She takes out the alethiometer.

PANTALAIMON What you doin'?

LYRA I'm gonna have one more go at finding Roger before she comes barging in. I been thinking. If I point the needles at the pictures round the outside … maybe that's part of asking the question.

Pantalaimon looks.

PANTALAIMON Point one of 'em at the moon.

LYRA Why the moon?

PANTALAIMON Because it disappears like Roger did.

LYRA Yeah, right. And the horse, for travel. And … what stands for 'Roger'?

PANTALAIMON Something to do with 'friend'.

LYRA The dolphin, 'cause dolphins are friendly.

The needles are all in place.

PANTALAIMON Go on.

LYRA 'Where's Roger?'

They watch.

PANTALAIMON That needle's moving.

LYRA Yeah! But it's not saying nothing, is it? It's just swinging around any old how.

Louder:

'Where's Roger?' Oh, Pan, it's stopped!

PANTALAIMON Look out.

The golden monkey appears, followed by Mrs Coulter. Lyra sneaks the alethiometer back into her shoulder bag.

MRS COULTER Lyra dear, you haven't been out, I hope?

LYRA No, I been in *all day*!

MRS COULTER I know I'm always saying this, and I'm sure you must find it very boring of me, but if you want to go out, you must do so with me or …

LYRA/MRS COULTER … with one of the servants.

MRS COULTER Exactly.

She rearranges flowers in a vase.

Now are you quite clear about what I want you to do at the party this evening?

LYRA I en't forgo'en.

MRS COULTER *Haven't* forgotten! Sound those 't's: 't', 't', 't'. I want you to circulate with the canapés and make agreeable conversation. There'll be some very important people here … friends of mine, and people in government and opinion-formers … and you must live up to their expectations.

LYRA They don't know nothin' about me.

MRS COULTER One can be better known than one is aware of.

LYRA How?

MRS COULTER Stop asking pointless questions and listen to what I'm trying to tell you. There is one guest in particular who'll be wanting to talk to you. His name is Boreal, Lord Boreal, and he's a spy for the Church, so it is very important indeed that you tell him you're happy in London and that you want to stay. Because the Church is just the tiniest bit cross with me for taking you away from Oxford.

She puts her arms round Lyra.

Yes, it's true. They'd rather you were stuck in that dreary college, where you could be stolen at any moment by … well, never mind who by. But I'm not going to let you go, my darling, and I'll tell you the reason.

She looks Lyra in the eye with great seriousness.

After the party, after the guests have gone, you and I and dear little Pantalaimon will sit down quietly, and I'll tell you about the work that I want you to do for the General Oblation Board. You're going to be, oh, so much more useful to it than any grown-up could be. You'll be meeting other children, less well-off than you, and you'll be giving them the chance to travel.

LYRA Will I go to the Arctic?

MRS COULTER If you do well, there will be *lots and lots* of reasons for you to go there. That's something to look forward to, isn't it?

Pantalaimon signals 'No'.

LYRA Yeah.

MRS COULTER So that's a promise. Now are you looking your best, I wonder? Up on your feet.

Lyra stands and Mrs Coulter inspects her from a distance.

Not bad. Not bad at all. But not the shoulder bag, of course. Will you take it off, please?

The golden monkey paws the shoulder bag.

LYRA Have I got to? I really like it. It's the only thing I've got that belongs to me.

MRS COULTER But Lyra, it looks absurd to wear a shoulder bag in one's own home. Take it off!

LYRA No!

She stamps her foot.

MRS COULTER I'll ask you one more time. Take off that bag. And never stamp your foot again, either in my sight or out of it.

LYRA Come on, Pan. Let's go.

She's about to go. The golden monkey springs on to Pantalaimon, pinning him to the ground. Lyra feels pain.

LYRA Stop hurting us! Please!

MRS COULTER *(calm)* I think you'll find that once you remove the bag, he'll let you go.

Lyra takes off the bag. The golden monkey releases Pantalaimon.

MRS COULTER Thank you. Kiss me.

Lyra does.

Now, have the caterers brought enough ice, do you think? Warm drinks are *horrid*.

She goes out. Lyra holds Pantalaimon close.

PANTALAIMON She's evil all through.

LYRA I hate her!

Guests arrive and the room is full. Lyra and Pantalaimon circulate with a tray of canapés. Mrs Coulter calls:

MRS COULTER Into the music room, everybody! Hurry!

The guests move out. Lord Boreal approaches Lyra.

LORD BOREAL Good evening, Lyra. Let's give the music room a miss, shall we? I'd greatly enjoy a moment's conversation. I'm Lord Boreal.

LYRA Yeah, I guessed.

LORD BOREAL Are you enjoying yourself in London?

LYRA Sort of.

LORD BOREAL And is Mrs Coulter keeping you fruitfully occupied? Busy, I mean?

LYRA Well, up to now it's just been going shopping and having my hair done, stuff like that. But soon, I'm gonna be helping the General Oblation Board.

LORD BOREAL Are you indeed?

LYRA Yeah, and I'm going to the Arctic.

LORD BOREAL So that's where she takes them, is it?

LYRA *(doubtfully)* Yeah, I s'pose it is.

LORD BOREAL What else have you learned about the General Oblation Board?

LYRA Well … I learned about children, of course. And Dust. And sacrifices. 'Cause that's what an oblate is, that's what I 'eard.

LORD BOREAL I'm delighted that Mrs Coulter has taken you into her confidence. Though 'sacrifice' is rather a melodramatic way of putting it. The children all come to her willingly, after all.

Lyra and Pantalaimon recoil in horror, but try to disguise their feelings.

She was worried, you know, that you might be grabbed off the streets by some over-enthusiastic helper of hers. That was the reason she brought you here. But I knew it would only be a matter of time before she made you a part of her collection team. A child to catch a child … and what a charming snippet of bait you'll be! It's surprising, isn't it, that no one has worked it out? 'General Oblation Board.' G.O.B. … and then …

LYRA … the Gobblers. Yes, it's *very* surprising.

Lord Boreal goes.

It's her!

PANTALAIMON Run for it!

She grabs the alethiometer and they climb out of the window. Mrs Coulter appears in the doorway.

MRS COULTER Lyra? Lyra, what are you doing? Come back at once!

Scene 8

Oxford: outside the Master's study. *There's a big pile of luggage outside the door. The Master comes out, carrying another suitcase. He locks the door, turns to go and, to his great alarm, sees Fra Pavel.*

MASTER Fra Pavel! I thought you were in Geneva.

FRA PAVEL What are you doing?

MASTER I'm going to Scotland. Just for the weekend.

He looks guiltily at the large pile of luggage.

No, the South Coast.

FRA PAVEL Nonsense. You're running away. Do you really suppose that you can flee the consequences of your actions? Your attempt on Lord Asriel's life was an abject farce. You let the college actually pay for his expedition. You gave Lyra into the hands of Mrs Coulter . . .

MASTER I thought it was what you wanted!

FRA PAVEL Did she tell you that?

MASTER No, not exactly. I was wrong. But …

FRA PAVEL Lyra has run away. The police can't find her, and neither can we. Even the Tartar guards are combing the streets to no avail.

MASTER I know all this, and I can't for the life of me see why everyone is going to such lengths to find a perfectly ordinary girl of twelve.

FRA PAVEL Ordinary? It has escaped your attention, then, that I have watched her, visited her twice a year ever since she was a baby?

MASTER I've never known why.

FRA PAVEL You have an alethiometer here at Jordan College, is that correct?

MASTER Why do you ask?

FRA PAVEL The Church has the only other example in the Western world. I'm its official reader. And it has warned me of a prophecy, a witches' prophecy, awesome and strange but true. A child of destiny will be born. The circumstances of Lyra's birth make clear that she is that child.

MASTER What *is* her destiny?

FRA PAVEL Lyra will either redeem the Church, will carry it on to greater glory … or she will destroy it. Which of the two it will be is a secret that only the witches know. Either way, our future depends on her. And now you know why it's imperative that she's found. Bring me the alethiometer.

MASTER You mean, the one that belongs to the college?

FRA PAVEL Obviously. Mine's in Geneva. What are you waiting for? Well?

MASTER Lyra has it. I gave it to her.

Fra Pavel lays a friendly hand on the Master's shoulder and attempts a pleasant smile.

FRA PAVEL Wait in your study. You will shortly receive a visit.

Scene 9

***London.** Night and fog. There's a late-night coffee stall. Lyra and Pantalaimon run on, closely followed by Tartar guards. They hide and the guards move on.*

LYRA Are they gone yet?

PANTALAIMON Yeah, they went slavering round the corner.

LYRA Don't cry, Pan. We'll find a place to sleep.

PANTALAIMON It's all so frightening.

LYRA Ssh. A nice ham sandwich would warm us up.

PANTALAIMON Do you think it's safe?

LYRA It better 'ad be, 'cause I'm starving.

They approach the coffee stall. A man in a top hat and a white silk muffler eyes Lyra in predatory fashion.

STALLHOLDER Yes, love?

LYRA Cup of coffee and an 'am sandwich, please.

PANTALAIMON Don't look round.

TOP-HATTED MAN You're out late, my dear.

PANTALAIMON Ignore him.

LYRA I *am* doing.

STALLHOLDER Here you are, me love. That'll be two groats.

TOP-HATTED MAN Allow me.

He pays.

LYRA Can I have more sugar?

STALLHOLDER Certainly, love.

The top-hatted man produces a brandy flask.

TOP-HATTED MAN Wouldn't you rather have some brandy in your coffee?

LYRA No, I don't like brandy.

TOP-HATTED MAN I'm sure you've never had brandy like this before.

PANTALAIMON I said, ignore him.

TOP-HATTED MAN And where are you going to, all alone?

LYRA I'm going to meet my father.

TOP-HATTED MAN Oh, your father? Is he someone very important?

LYRA Yes, he's a murderer.

TOP-HATTED MAN A what?

LYRA A murderer. It's his job. He's doing a murder tonight. I got his soap and a clean towel in here, 'cause he's usually all covered in blood when he's finished. There he is now. He looks a bit angry.

The top-hatted man backs away and disappears.

PANTALAIMON Lyra the liar!

LYRA Got rid of him, though, didn' I?

PANTALAIMON *Now* where're we going?

LYRA Dunno. We'll find a derelict house or summat.

A security light flashes on and a siren blows. Two Tartars appear with wolf daemons. Lyra and Pantalaimon run and are nearly caught. Tony Costa's voice is heard:

TONY Lyra!

One of the Tartars collapses, shot with an arrow. The other is felled by a second arrow. Tony Costa and his fellow gyptian Ben run on, armed with bows and arrows.

TONY Don't scream! It's me!

LYRA Who?

TONY Tony. Tony Costa, Billy's brother. From Oxford, remember? When you threw mud at our boat? And told me some daft tale about a skeleton what done it?

LYRA Oh Tony, I'm sorry!

TONY Aye well, never mind about that now. We stumbled across you just in time, and that's what matters. This is my mate Ben, best bow-and-arrow man in the gyptian nation.

BEN Tartar warriors, those were. Come on, let's not hang about. Our pals'll be waiting for us on board.

LYRA Where are you going, Tony?

TONY Well, this is a secret, lass …

BEN Aye, keep it dark. They've got eyes and ears all over the shop, them Gobblers.

TONY But Lyra here was a mate of Billy's, so it's right that she knows.

To Lyra:

Billy and Roger and all the rest of the stolen kids are gonna be rescued.

LYRA Rescued?

TONY Aye, there's a ship at harbour, leaving at midnight, under the captaincy of Lord John Faa himself, the Lord of the Western gyptians. And we're sailing it up to the Arctic, to find them kids and to bring 'em back home!

BEN Look after yourself.

TONY Aye, stay out of trouble.

They start to go.

LYRA Oh, Tony, listen … I saw a photogram of a man in the snow with his hand held up, like this … like he was calling me to the Arctic … and Lord Asriel's there, and Roger too, that I swore to rescue. I'm comin' with you!

TONY Never!

BEN Forget it!

LYRA I bloody am!

The interior of a ***rusty old hulk****. John Faa is there with other gyptians, among whom is the aged Farder Coram. Lyra comes in with Pan.*

JOHN FAA Now where had you got to, gal?

LYRA I been up on deck, Lord Faa. Pan was trying out being a dolphin, chasing the fish about, wasn't you, Pan?

JOHN FAA Come on in and sit yourself quietly. Friends, pay heed.

The gyptians settle and listen.

You all of you know how we gyptians suffered a lot worse than most from the Gobblers …

1ST GYPTIAN Except for the foreigner kids and the homeless kids.

2ND GYPTIAN Aye, they're crafty, them Gobblers.

JOHN FAA You're right. They are. And we was stuck for a way to fight back at 'em, till Tony and Ben here captured a Gobbler. We don't need to know what they done to 'im, but he talked all right. Lads, tell 'em.

TONY He said they take the kids up to the North … and they've got a laboratory there, kind of a hospital thing. And they …

He falters.

BEN Go on, Tony.

TONY Well … they do experiments on 'em.

1ST GYPTIAN What kind of experiments?

TONY He said, like … like cutting 'em up.

All are horrified.

2ND GYPTIAN You mean they kill them?

3RD GYPTIAN Or torture 'em?

BEN We don't know. That were the last he said.

JOHN FAA When I heard that news, I took the advice of Farder Coram here, who is a seer and a spirit-talker, and as wise as a tree of owls, and we called on the whole of the gyptian nation for men and for gold, for to charter this ship with.

He unrolls a map.

This is where we will shortly arrive. The port of Trollesund, on the southernmost tip of the land of ice.

2ND GYPTIAN Is that where the Gobblers are?

JOHN FAA It's where they land. Their laboratory is further away across the snows, we don't know where. We've got to find that out in Trollesund, along of getting what else we need. Guns, on top of our wretched knives and arrows. Some kind of fighting machine, to match with theirs, and transport too. Once we're fully equipped, we'll leave this child in a place of safety, and we'll march to the Gobblers' hideout.

There's a chorus of agreement, but:

LYRA No, that en't right. 'Cause I gotta go there with you.

She continues against a chorus of refusals:

I know all about the Gobblers, 'cause they tried to turn me into one of 'em. Please!

FARDER CORAM I say … let's take her with us.

JOHN FAA Farder Coram, will you briefly explain your reasoning?

FARDER CORAM That I will.

All listen.

The roads of chance are long and winding. Them as follows 'em oft-times lose their way …

JOHN FAA Briefly, briefly!

FARDER CORAM It's all to the point, but I'll jump to the nub of it. When I was in Oxford, Lyra, I heard that the Master give you an object that can help us on our journey. May I see it? Look in my eyes, and see if you trust me.

Lyra takes out the alethiometer and shows it to him.

Three little wheels, a circle of pictures and a compass-needle. It's an alethiometer all right. I seen one in China-land many years back. Do you know how to ask it questions?

LYRA Sort of.

FARDER CORAM And can you sort of read the answers?

LYRA No, not really …

JOHN FAA Farder Coram, with all due deference to your age and wisdom, if she can't work this thing, then it's no more use to us than a busted alarm clock.

FARDER CORAM I say we give her a test. Lyra?

LYRA All right. I'll ask it if I'm really safe from Mrs Coulter … or if she'll find me.

The men watch sceptically as she sets the needles.

The Madonna for her, and the baby for me, and this dragon thing, 'cause that means searching … well, it's one of the meanings.

She holds it in front of her like a microphone.

'Will Mrs Coulter find me?'

She looks at the dial. The gyptians get impatient.

JOHN FAA Well?

LYRA I'm trying!

Louder:

'Will Mrs Coulter find me? Will she … '

FARDER CORAM Lyra, if you yell at it like a drunken donkey-driver, it'll tell you nothing. It's got feelings, just like we have. Sit yourself easy. Let your mind go free … halfway between sleeping and waking … like being a needle floating on a glass of water. And when the answer comes, reach down … and further down, till you find the level.

Lyra relaxes.

LYRA It's moving! Yeah … The thunderbolt … twice at the baby… and a serpent an' a thing like a lizard with big pop eyes … and three times at the elephant. I got it! She's sending … a thing to find me … up in the air, I think … yes, flyin', flyin' an' spyin', nasty, angry, lock it up fast … and arrivin' soon. No, now. Right now. It's here.

The gyptians look round.

1ST GYPTIAN I can't see it.

2ND GYPTIAN Nor me.

3RD GYPTIAN Still waiting.

JOHN FAA Back to business. Lyra, go and play over there.

Suddenly a tiny whizzing object flies into view. The gyptians yell out and scatter. Ben traps it in a beer glass, where it rattles around trying to escape.

BEN I got it! I got it!

JOHN FAA What in the devil's name is it?

FARDER CORAM It's a spy-fly, John, sent snooping after us by the Gobbler woman. Get it in your smoke-leaf tin. Be careful!

Someone does and he manoeuvres the spy-fly into it.

It's built of clockwork that won't never run out, and pinned to the spring, there's a bad spirit with a spell through its heart. This thing's so monstrous angry at being cooped up, that if it ever got out, it'd tear and rip and slash the first creature it come across. And Lyra warned us!

LYRA What did I tell you? I can read it!

4TH GYPTIAN Land ahoy!

Scene 10

***Trollesund.** Unfriendly Trollesunders watch as the gyptians arrive.*

JOHN FAA We better get out by nightfall. Tony and Ben, you go into town. Ask whoever will talk to you, have they seen any kids and where did the Gobblers take 'em. Jake and Barnaby, look around town for all the firearms you can lay your hands on. Farder Coram, you take Lyra back to the ship for safety. *(to Lyra)* Don't move one step from there. The rest of you, help me look to our transportation.

All go but Lyra and Farder Coram.

FARDER CORAM I'm off into town meself. I've got a message to send to a notable witch from around these parts.

LYRA A *witch*?

FARDER CORAM Oh aye, and a powerful one, who just might lend us a hand. You do exactly as Lord Faa told you, you hear me?

He goes.

LYRA Come on.

She and Pantalaimon move on.

PANTALAIMON What're we doing?

LYRA We're gonna be helpful.

PANTALAIMON Like finding kids?

LYRA Yeah, kids'd be good. Or clues. Or Gobblers, even. Or …

She sees something.

PANTALAIMON What?

LYRA I can't *believe* it!

PANTALAIMON *What?*

LYRA You remember what Mrs Coulter said was the bravest fighter on earth? Well, look what we found!

Iorek comes into view. He's breaking up a big iron buoy.

PANTALAIMON An armoured bear!

LYRA That's right. He can fight for *us*.

PANTALAIMON He hasn't got no armour.

LYRA He must have taken it off to work.

PANTALAIMON He looks a wreck.

A bear-keeper appears with a bottle of spirits, which he nervously pushes towards Iorek with a stick. Iorek drinks from the bottle.

Oh-oh. He's a drunk as well.

LYRA He's still an armoured bear, though, isn't he? Let's go and get him.

She moves forward.

PANTALAIMON *Get* him? What're you talking about? He'll bite your head off!

Lyra approaches Iorek. Pantalaimon follows fearfully. Iorek glares at Lyra.

PANTALAIMON Not so close!

Lyra moves deliberately to within Iorek's reach.

IOREK Who are you?

LYRA I'm Lyra Belacqua and I got a job to offer you.

IOREK I've got a job.

LYRA This is a better one. An' I can pay you. I got three gold dollars.

IOREK I don't need gold. I need meat and spirits, and these people pay me plenty of both.

LYRA Yes, I can see that. You've got empty bottles all round you. You even *smell* of drink. Haven't you got any self-respect?

IOREK None.

PANTALAIMON Let's go.

LYRA Shuddup! ***(to Iorek)*** Don't you even want to know what I want you to do? It's fighting. It's fighting the people who come to Trollesund with their stolen kids.

IOREK I've seen those people. They're called the child-cutters. I hate them. But I can't fight them for you.

LYRA Why?

IOREK Because I can't fight anyone.

LYRA Why?

Iorek roars in desperation.

IOREK Because I've got no armour!

LYRA There's all this metal lying around. Why don't you make some armour out of that?

IOREK It's useless to me. I made my armour out of iron that fell from the skies in a trail of flame. Without it, I am nothing. I cannot go to war, and war is the sea I swim in and the air I breathe. My armour is my soul, just like your daemon is your soul. And it's been taken from me.

LYRA Who by?

IOREK The humans of this town. They gave me spirits to drink until I fell asleep, and then they took my armour away from me. I tried to find it, but I couldn't, so I went mad with rage. Now I must work in this yard until I have paid for the buildings I broke and the people I killed.

Lyra takes out the alethiometer.

LYRA I've got a machine that can answer questions. If I can find out where they've hidden your armour …

IOREK Then I'll fight your enemies and I'll serve you until I die. And I'll never drink spirits again.

LYRA But you mustn't hurt anyone if I ask you not to. Do you promise me on your honour?

IOREK On my honour.

LYRA All right, I'll ask.

She sets and reads the alethiometer.

LYRA It's in the house of the priest.

Iorek raises himself up and roars in frustration.

IOREK I want to get it now!

LYRA Why don't you?

IOREK Because I promised to work till sunset!

LYRA If you're as small as me, it's sunset now. Look.

Iorek crouches to her height.

IOREK You're right.

He roars and bounds away.

LYRA We've got him!

The gyptians appear, with Farder Coram and John Faa among them.

BEN This town is evil! Evil!

2ND GYPTIAN Let's just get out!

SEVERAL Aye! Out!

1ST GYPTIAN We asked the priest, had he seen any kids, and he set his bloody dogs on us!

He shows a rip in his trousers.

3RD GYPTIAN You brung us to hell, Lord Faa, where there en't no hope of travelling further on!

2ND GYPTIAN Aye, where're we goin'? Where? Where?

FARDER CORAM Friends, listen to me!

They fall silent and listen.

When the present is dark and the future is yet unknown, it is the long-betided past which …

The gyptians groan in frustration.

All right, I'll jump to the practical bit. I sent a message, friends, to Serafina Pekkala, the Queen of the Lapland witches, and a long-lost friend of my youth-time days. She's sent us a creature to guide us, and here he is.

He calls upwards.

Kaisa!

Kaisa, a snow goose, appears and lands.

KAISA Farder Coram! It's lucky you called. I wouldn't have recognised you in a month of Sundays.

The gyptians stare at it in alarm.

2ND GYPTIAN It's a daemon!

3RD GYPTIAN But there en't no human attached!

FARDER CORAM Friends, have no fear! This kind and intelligent snow goose is Serafina Pekkala's very own daemon. For witches, you see, can send their daemons a whole sight further than what we can. Tell me, Kaisa, is your mistress still young and beautiful?

KAISA She is, and she remembers you as handsome as ever you were.

A knowing sigh of 'Ah's' arises from the gyptians.

FARDER CORAM Well it were a long time ago. *(to Kaisa)* Does she know where the children are?

KAISA Indeed she does, and I've been sent to guide you!

JOHN FAA What kind of a place have the Gobblers taken them to?

KAISA It's the worst of places. We don't know what they do there, but there's hatred and fear for miles around. Even the little lemmings and foxes keep their distance. That's why it is called 'Bolvangar'. 'Fields of evil.'

LYRA Is a boy called Roger there?

KAISA Who is this child?

LYRA I'm Lyra Belacqua.

KAISA Lyra Belacqua? My queen will be mightily interested to know you've come.

LYRA Why?

KAISA Because of Lord Asriel, and his plan to travel between the worlds.

LYRA Like to the city in the Northern Lights?

KAISA That world is one, but there are many … many … others. They are not in our universe, but they're here, right next to us, close as a heartbeat, linked with the world we know. I spread my wings …

He spreads his wings.

… and brush ten million other worlds, and they know nothing of it. Tell me, Lyra …

The bear-keeper appears, followed by the Mayor and angry townspeople.

BEAR-KEEPER That's the girl, your worship! She was whispering to the bear, and he went rampaging off!

MAYOR Gyptians! Gyptians! Always the same!

JOHN FAA What's goin' on?

LYRA I found a bear, and he's gonna come with us, that's what.

The gyptians are alarmed.

GYPTIANS A bear?

JOHN FAA Lyra, what in the name of all that's wonderful made you think we wanted a bear?

MAYOR *(to John Faa)* Oh you know nothing about it, I suppose?

He continues, while the townspeople chip in with insults and the gyptians answer with abuse.

That bear is ours! You've got no right to him, none. It's not two weeks since he went roaring drunken around the town, tore down the bank and the police station too, not to mention three innocent citizens lying dead as a doornail in the street!

JOHN FAA Oh Lyra, Lyra!

LYRA They'd stolen his armour! It's only natural that he got a bit annoyed. Please let's take him! He'll be a wonderful fighter. He's fierce, he's strong.

JOHN FAA Lyra, he's as likely to kill us as he is the Gobblers.

LYRA He's not! He won't hurt anyone if I ask him not to. He's given me his word of honour.

JOHN FAA Honour? That's a human thing. What's a bear know about honour?

LYRA I looked in his eyes and I trusted him. I could see it, Lord Faa.

There is a loud crash as of a wooden house being knocked down. The priest rushes into view. Iorek appears in his rusty armour. Everyone scatters. Iorek chases the Mayor and is about to knock off his head when:

LYRA No, Iorek! Don't do it!

Iorek backs away.

MAYOR Put this beast in chains!

LYRA Don't you bloody dare!

Men advance with chains. A shot rings out and a man's hat flies off.

MAYOR Who did that?

Lee Scoresby appears with his rifle. His daemon is Hester, a hare.

HESTER We did. Back off.

JOHN FAA Who are you?

LEE SCORESBY Scoresby's the name, Texan by birth, sharpshooter by profession, temporarily stranded here with my balloon-for-hire and a cargo of rifles, owing to a certain local prospecting outfit that never paid my fee.

He flashes the Mayor a dirty look.

HESTER Howdy, Iorek.

IOREK Hello, Hester. Hello, Lee!

Lee and Iorek embrace.

JOHN FAA Do you know this bear?

LEE SCORESBY Sure do. Iorek Byrnison an' me fought in the Tungusk campaign together. He's an awkward critter, and he ain't exactly looking his best right now, but give him a wash and a brush-up, and he'll be the greatest fighter that you ever saw.

JOHN FAA So what would you think to him joining our rescue expedition?

LEE SCORESBY Take me too and I might consider it.

HESTER Not so fast. What'll you pay?

JOHN FAA One hundred dollars for the two of you.

HESTER *(outraged)* One hundred dollars! That's ridiculous!

LEE SCORESBY Done.

He shakes John Faa's hand. Applause. John Faa addresses the gyptians.

JOHN FAA Friends! We're fit and set and ready to go.

He raises his hammer.

Let's march!

GYPTIANS Aye! To the rescue! To Bolvangar!

Lyra and the gyptians set off through ***the Northern snows.*** *Iorek pounds alongside them and Kaisa flies ahead, as guide. After a while:*

JOHN FAA Halt! We're close enough. Here's where we'll stop for the night.

Gyptians point upwards and call:

GYPTIANS Look out! Spy-fly!

KAISA Have no fear! I'll head it off, and meet you all at our destination. Farewell!

The gyptians bid him farewell as he flies out of sight.

JOHN FAA Get some sleep now, boys. We got a big day tomorrow.

They all settle down for the night.

BEN *(to Lyra)* Stay here, gal. I'll get you something warm to keep the chill out.

He goes to get her a blanket. John Faa approaches.

JOHN FAA I've been thinking, Lyra, that your symbol-reader thingummy could be useful. First thing in the morning, ask it how many Gobbler soldiers are there. I'll come and help you.

He goes.

LYRA *Help!* What a cheek.

PANTALAIMON Ask it now.

Lyra consults the alethiometer.

LYRA It's saying that there's a Gobbler place quite near, with Tartar warriors. And they're guarding something. It's strange … it's like a child, but it isn't a child.

PANTALAIMON Maybe it's Roger.

LYRA Yeah! Let's go and look, when they're all asleep.

Iorek appears carrying a little metal box.

What's that?

IOREK Farder Coram asked me to put his smoke-leaf tin into something stronger. Keep it for him.

Lyra takes it.

LYRA It's beautiful.

IOREK We armoured bears are skilled in working with metal. And I can do more than any bear alive. What is inside this?

LYRA An angry spirit.

She puts it to her ear.

Very angry. Mrs Coulter sent it after me.

Iorek is horrified and amazed.

IOREK Mrs Coulter? Do you know her?

LYRA Yes! She's my worst enemy! What's she got to do with you?

IOREK She is the woman who destroyed me. If it wasn't for her, I would still be the king of Svalbard, home of the armoured bears.

LYRA What did she do to you?

IOREK I had a rival, Iofur Raknison, a bear of enormous strength, but vain and treacherous. Mrs Coulter plotted with him against me and I was cast out of Svalbard to wander the Arctic like a vagrant, till I came to Trollesund.

LYRA Yeah, she's bad enough for that.

IOREK There's more. Iofur Raknison seized the throne of Svalbard. He pulled down our ancient fortress of ice and built a palace of stone and marble. Then Mrs Coulter promised to get him a daemon – as though he were a human being! Once that thought was planted in his crafty brain, he could never get rid of it. Now he dreams of daemons, talks of daemons, longs for a daemon. Worst of all …

LYRA What?

IOREK … she did all this, not from some foolish desire to improve our lives. She just wanted gaolers.

LYRA *Gaolers?*

IOREK Mrs Coulter had an enemy. She wanted him kept a prisoner in the strongest fortress ever known, guarded by the stubbornest creatures on earth. So she brought Lord Asriel to the castle of Svalbard, and they threw him in chains.

LYRA *Lord Asriel!*

IOREK Do you know Lord Asriel *too*?

LYRA Yes, he's my uncle! Iorek, listen! Once we've rescued Roger, and all the kids, we'll go to Svalbard. We'll free Lord Asriel, and we'll win your throne back, and …

IOREK Do you think, if that were possible, that I wouldn't have done it already? Iofur Raknison has an army of five hundred bears, each as mighty as me …

LYRA Then we'll trick him.

Iorek laughs and shakes his head.

IOREK No one can trick a bear.

LYRA *You* were tricked by the people in Trollesund.

IOREK I drank spirits. That's a human thing to do. If I'd been true to my bear-like nature, they would never have got the better of me. Bears can see deceit, we see it as plain as arms and legs. It's a gift we were born with. Just as you have a gift. You can read your truth-telling machine, but grown-ups can't. As you are to them, so am I to a human being.

LYRA So when I'm a grown-up … will I not be able to read it?

IOREK There is a different kind of gift that comes with learning. Bears don't have it.

He yawns enormously.

I must rest.

He goes. Lyra looks at the spy-fly box, puts it away.

LYRA Let's go look for Roger.

They creep quietly away and through the snows.

I know what we gotta do now. Once we've rescued him and the kids, we'll go to Svalbard, and I'll free Lord Asriel. And I'll use the alethiometer to set him free. And then he'll thank me, won't he? He won't be calling me bothersome or disgusting. And he'll …

PANTALAIMON Forget it.

LYRA Why?

PANTALAIMON 'Cause you can't trick bears.

LYRA You can't trick bears as long as they're true to their bear-like nature. But Iofur Rakniwhatsit's trying to be a human being, isn't he? So maybe he's trickable. And maybe … Oh-oh.

*They've reached a **Tartar camp**. Tartar guards with wolves patrol it.*

PANTALAIMON Tartars.

LYRA Ssh. This way.

They slip past the guards and creep on to a seemingly empty space.

PANTALAIMON There's nothing here.

LYRA Look.

A small figure can be seen a distance away from them.

LYRA Roger? Rodge, is it you?

The figure becomes clearer as it turns towards them. It's Billy Costa. He looks white, drained and half-alive and speaks in a feeble whisper.

BILLY You seen my Ratter?

LYRA That ain't Rodge. It's Billy Costa. Billy, what's wrong?

Pantalaimon, very alarmed, approaches Billy and searches all around him.

PANTALAIMON *He's got no daemon!*

BILLY Ratter. I lost my Ratter.

LYRA Oh Billy, what happened?

BILLY Ratter? Ratter?

He collapses. Tartar guards appear with their wolves. They put a sack over Lyra's head and bundle her away.

Scene 11

***Bolvangar**. Searchlights, a high fence, a watch-tower. The Tartar guards deliver Lyra to a nurse. She has a spooky, robotic manner of speech.*

NURSE Welcome to Bolvangar. What is your name?

PANTALAIMON *(very quietly)* Don't tell 'er.

LYRA It's Lizzie. Lizzie Brooks.

NURSE Hello, Lizzie. Have you come a long way? That coat will need a wash. Let's change it.

She starts putting Lyra into an institutional gown.

We'll put your shoulder bag in your very own locker. What's inside it? Let's see.

She discovers the spy-fly box.

Oh dear. A funny old box.

She finds the alethiometer.

And what's this? A compass? We'll get you something pretty and soft to play with, like a doll or a nice woolly bear.

LYRA I want them back. And I'm keeping that bag as well.

NURSE All right. Follow me.

She hands them back.

You have arrived in time for recreation.

*She leads Lyra to the **recreation area**. Girls are playing apathetically with a skipping rope.*

PANTALAIMON I'm too frightened to look. Have they all got daemons?

LYRA Yeah, don't worry.

She joins the other girls.

Hello.

LILY Hello.

LYRA I'm Lizzie.

LILY Hello, Lizzie.

LYRA What's going on?

LILY Nothing much.

DAISY It's just boring really. They give us tests, and then they lie us down and they take our temperature.

LYRA Yeah, it sounds pretty boring.

DAISY They're always going on about our daemons. Finding out how heavy they are an' all. They got a weighing machine, and your daemon gets on to it, and then they write things down and take his photo.

LILY But it's the Dust they're measuring.

DAISY Yeah, they talk about Dust non-stop.

JESSIE I en't dusty. I had a shower yesterday.

DAISY It isn't that kind of dust. It's Special Dust. Every grown-up gets it in the end. That's what *she* says.

JESSIE The pretty lady.

LILY Mrs Coulter.

LYRA Is she here now?

JESSIE She *wasn't*, but she's coming today to look at a new machine.

The nurse appears with the boys. Roger is among them.

NURSE Hurry along!

DAISY Here's the boys.

JESSIE We're not supposed to talk to 'em, but some of us manage!

They laugh.

NURSE Girls! No smiling!

Roger and Lyra see each other.

LYRA Rodge!

NURSE No talking to the girls! Play with the ball.

The nurse exits. Roger and Lyra manoeuvre themselves into contact.

ROGER I can't *believe* it! How did you *get* here?

LYRA I worked it out. It weren't that difficult really. Are you all right?

ROGER No, I never been so frightened ever. It weren't so bad when Billy was here. Then last week they Read 'Is Name Out.

LYRA What'ya mean?

ROGER They Read Your Name Out, and you gotta go with 'em. There's one boy says that they give you an operation, an' he heard what a nurse was saying. She said to a kid, we're not going to kill your daemon or nothing, it's only a cut. But I en't seen Billy anywhere, not since then. Look out!

The nurse returns with another nurse.

NURSE Children, listen carefully. In a few moments we will have a fire drill.

The fire alarm goes.

That is the fire alarm. Go outside to the assembly point and await further instructions. Off you go.

2ND NURSE Assembly point! Assembly point!

The children follow the nurses off. Lyra and Roger hide.

ROGER Where we goin'?

LYRA Where they can't see us.

They reach a ***building*** *with a large red sign on the door: ENTRY STRICTLY FORBIDDEN.*

Listen, Rodge. There's a whole load of gyptians coming to rescue us any minute from now.

ROGER Honest?

LYRA Yeah! And it en't just gyptians neither. There's an armoured bear, an' a man who flies a balloon from Texas an' a witch's daemon, only there en't no witch.

Roger is very upset.

ROGER Oh, Lyra! What an 'orrible trick to play!

He continues as Kaisa appears and lands.

You come all this way, an' then all you can do is make up stories! Lyra the liar!

He sees Kaisa.

KAISA Greetings, Lyra.

LYRA Greetings to you, Kaisa!

ROGER It's true!

LYRA I told you. Where's the gyptians?

KAISA There's been a small delay.

LYRA Oh no!

KAISA It seems the spy-fly had reported their position. The better news is that Serafina Pekkala and her band of witches are coming to join the battle. May I suggest that this young gentleman prepares the children for a rapid escape?

ROGER That me?

PANTALAIMON Tell them we're gonna set off the fire alarm …

KAISA That's very good thinking, Pantalaimon.

LYRA … yeah, an' then they all gotta run outside … and take their coats and boots and stuff or they'll freeze to death. Go on.

Roger goes.

KAISA You must hide. Mrs Coulter's coming over the brow of the hill in a dog sleigh.

Lyra sees the forbidden door.

LYRA I'll go in there.

Pantalaimon whimpers.

PANTALAIMON No, don't!

KAISA What's the matter, Pantalaimon?

PANTALAIMON I have a very unpleasant reaction to that door.

Voices are heard. Dr Cade: 'She went this way.' Dr West: 'Yes, here are her footprints!'

LYRA I gotta go somewhere!

She opens the door. It swings open, revealing a cage filled with severed daemons, pressing their faces to the wire and howling. Pantalaimon leaps into Lyra's arms.

KAISA Where are the children of these daemons?

LYRA They've been cut away. That's what they do! They're cutting their daemons away!

PANTALAIMON Save them! Save them!

KAISA There is no saving to be done. They're lost for ever. Go!

He flies off. Two doctors appear and grab Lyra.

DR WEST This is the girl!

DR CADE What's going on here?

He closes the door.

DR WEST What have you seen? What have you seen?

LYRA Leave me alone!

PANTALAIMON Let her go!

DR CADE We can't let her go back to the other children. She'll blurt it all out, and we'll have total panic all round.

DR WEST There's only one thing we *can* do, it seems to me.

DR CADE What, now?

DR WEST Why not?

DR CADE But Mrs Coulter hasn't arrived. I thought she had to be there for each experiment.

DR WEST That's what she *says* … but there's no scientific justification for it. She simply enjoys watching.

DR CADE Then we just won't tell her. The shock will certainly prevent the girl from talking. Where's Doctor Sargent?

DR WEST In the laboratory.

*They enter a **laboratory**. Dr Sargent is there. There's a machine with an operating chair, a small cage and a guillotine blade between the two. Lyra is thrown on to the chair. Dr West puts on plastic gloves.*

DR SARGENT Gentlemen, what very good timing. May we position the subject?

PANTALAIMON What are you doing!

DR SARGENT It's just this moment that I've brought the apparatus up to the testing stage. Now the daemon please.

Dr West grabs Pantalaimon and puts him in the cage. The parting is agonising for both him and Lyra. She screams:

LYRA You can't touch him! You can't touch him!

DR SARGENT Reveal the daemon bond, Dr West.

DR WEST Coming right up!

The bond between Lyra and Pantalaimon is made visible.

DR SARGENT Dr Cade, are you standing by with the resuscitation equipment?

DR CADE I am.

PANTALAIMON Lyra! Lyra!

LYRA Pan!

DR SARGENT *(to Lyra)* Keep still for a moment for me, if you would. That's perfect.

The blade is about to fall. Mrs Coulter appears.

MRS COULTER Stop!

She recognises Lyra.

Lyra! Let that child out this instant!

The junior doctors release Lyra and Pantalaimon.

DR SARGENT But Mrs Coulter …

MRS COULTER No experiments may take place when I am not in attendance. I must see each one.

DR SARGENT But …

MRS COULTER Each one! Now get out! Get out!

The doctors go. Mrs Coulter embraces Lyra, who is crying.

Oh Lyra, Lyra. Poor, poor child. It's all right now. Don't cry.

LYRA Oh, Pan!

She embraces Pantalaimon.

MRS COULTER What trouble you've caused. I was beside myself. I've never been so upset. I searched for you all through London.

LYRA You sent the Tartars after me, and the spy-flies too.

MRS COULTER I had to, darling. Once I knew you were with those ruffian gyptians … and a fine job they made of looking after you. Just think what would have happened if I had arrived a moment later.

LYRA Why do you do it? How can you be so cruel?

MRS COULTER Lyra, Lyra, it may *seem* cruel. But it's for scientific progress … and the betterment of humanity … and yes, for the child's own good. Just one little cut, and then it's safe from Dust for ever after.

LYRA What's wrong with Dust?

MRS COULTER Why, everything's wrong, my dearest. Dust is evil and wicked. It doesn't collect around sweet and innocent children … but just a little bit later, at what we call the age of puberty? When your daemon settles? Then Dust clusters around you, radiates to and from you … and the innocent child begins to have all sorts of nasty thoughts and feelings. And all it takes to stop them happening, is a snip. A tiny snip. The daemon isn't killed. It's simply not connected. It's like a sweet little pet.

LYRA If cutting's so good, then why did you stop them doing it to me? You should have been glad!

MRS COULTER Darling, these are grown-up thoughts.

LYRA They're not! There isn't a kid in the whole world that wouldn't ask you exactly the same thing. 'Cause you'd have done it to Roger, and he's my friend. And you did it to Billy Costa, and I saw him, he's no more'n a ghost!

MRS COULTER But, Lyra, you aren't Billy or Roger. You're … you're …

LYRA What?

Mrs Coulter looks at her thoughtfully.

MRS COULTER What did they tell you at Jordan College, about where you came from?

LYRA Came from?

MRS COULTER I'm asking about your mother and father.

LYRA They said they was killed in an airship accident.

MRS COULTER *Were* killed. Except they weren't. Your father was … and is … a remarkable man. He …

LYRA You mean he's alive?

MRS COULTER He is. He's … Well, I suppose you have to find out some day. He's Lord Asriel.

LYRA What?

MRS COULTER You didn't know?

LYRA No! Lord Asriel? He's my dad? That's *incredible*. And he escaped the airship accident? Yeah, he would. He's ever so clever. But … you put him in prison!

MRS COULTER Lyra …!

LYRA You put my father into a stinky dungeon!

MRS COULTER I had no choice. Let me finish my story before you condemn and reject me.

LYRA Well?

MRS COULTER The airship accident never happened. It was just a story that Lord Asriel invented to deny the facts of the matter. He loved your mother and she loved him. It was a wonderful love. But she was married already. And when you were born, her husband guessed the truth, and Lord Asriel fought him and killed him. No one ever denied that the fight was a fair one, not even at the trial.

LYRA The *trial*?

MRS COULTER There was a trial for murder. And the end of it was that Lord Asriel had to give up his estates, his palaces, his enormous wealth … though your mother, of course, knew nothing about this. She was so distressed by all that had happened that … that she wasn't even able to look after you. And that's when Lord Asriel did something very wrong and cruel. He put you into the care of Jordan College, and he told the Master that your mother should never be allowed to have anything to do with you. She was banned and shunned from being with her very own daughter. And that's how things stayed until she came to Jordan College and spoke to the Master …

LYRA You mean that …?

MRS COULTER Yes.

LYRA You can't be.

MRS COULTER I am. I'm your mother. Do you understand now why I put your father in prison? It was my only chance to be with you, to hug you and love you, to talk to you frankly as woman to woman. But you're exhausted, poor child. I'll put you to bed. Oh yes. There's just one tiny thing that I have to ask you. The Master told me ... before his tragic accident ... that he gave you a certain toy.

Lyra freezes.

It's called an 'alethiometer'. Shall I look after it for you?

After a moment's thought, Lyra takes out the spy-fly tin and hands it to Mrs Coulter.

Oh, you're keeping it safe in here. Thank you. It's a beautiful little tin ... not easy to open, though.

She finds a scalpel. The golden monkey watches as she cuts.

I'm longing to see what it looks like. Here we are.

With a furious buzz, the spy-fly shoots out and crashes into the monkey's face. Mrs Coulter is injured by proxy. Crashes and explosions are heard. Roger rushes into view.

ROGER Lyra! Come on! The kids are waiting!

Lyra sets off the fire alarm, and she, Roger and Pantalaimon run out . . . ***into the snow****. Children are there, waving excitedly as the gyptians approach. Tartar guards, doctors and nurses appear and attack the gyptians. Iorek drives off Tartar guards, and Lee fires at individuals with deadly aim. The gyptians rescue the children. Roger points to the skies:*

ROGER Look!

Serafina Pekkala appears on the roof.

SERAFINA Lyra Belacqua!

LYRA Who are you?

SERAFINA I'm Serafina Pekkala! Seize my hand! We're flying to Svalbard!

Lyra grabs Serafina with one hand and Roger with the other. Mrs Coulter appears with her golden monkey. Both are wounded in the same place. Mrs Coulter extends her arms upwards.

MRS COULTER Lyra!

Act Two

Scene 1

Oxford/Oxford: the* Botanic Gardens*. Night.* Will *and* Lyra *as before.

WILL So … while you were ballooning over the icebergs, I was standing … trying very hard not to be noticed … at a bus shelter in Oxford. It was midnight and I'd killed a man. I'd actually killed him. I'd heard the thwack of his head as it hit the floor. And I'd run, I'd pelted down the stairs and legged it into the night. With this. This green leather case that started it all.

LYRA What I understand much better now, is how many different forces were moving us on.

WILL I knew the cops'd be after me. By the morning there wouldn't be a single police car buzzing past that didn't have my name and photo.

LYRA There was what I wanted. And there was what you wanted. And there was what the grown-ups wanted, which was mostly completely different. But there was also … something bigger than all of us put together …

WILL I didn't know what they did to twelve year-old murderers, but it wouldn't be nice …

LYRA … like an enormous wind, sweeping us forwards …

WILL … and while I was standing … shaking with fear … I saw a window in the air. We saw so many of 'em after that, but that first time is the one I remember best. I looked, and there was Cittàgazze.

LYRA … taking us to places we didn't even know existed.

WILL There were little waterside shops and cafés and the smell of the sea and a warm wind …

LYRA Our fate …

WILL … and palm trees.

LYRA … our destiny.

WILL So I went through.

Scene 2

In the basket of Lee Scoresby's balloon. ***Serafina Pekkala, on her branch of cloud-pine, tows the balloon. Lyra, Iorek and Roger are out of sight, asleep in the basket.***

SERAFINA Are the children asleep down there?

LEE SCORESBY They sure are, and Iorek too. It looks like they won't wake up till we get there.

SERAFINA It won't be long now. See that black line ahead of us? That's the Svalbard cliffs. We'll have to keep our height as we fly over them, or the cliff-ghasts will be swooping up after us all, and me in particular. They've a great liking for witch-flesh.

LEE SCORESBY Can't you make yourself invisible?

SERAFINA I can empty my head of thought so that a short-lived mortal won't *notice* me. That's not invisible, quite, and it wouldn't prevail against cliff-ghasts. They have no human sensitivities for me to cancel out, just hates and appetites. And what will you do, Mr Scoresby, once we've landed?

LEE SCORESBY I'll set down Iorek and the kids, and I'll find a wind to blow me back to Trollesund. Landing Iorek in the other bear's kingdom could count as an act of war. And like I told that critter, one bear against five hundred isn't a war. It's plain suicide.

SERAFINA But Iorek has sworn to stay with Lyra until he dies, and that he will do.

LEE SCORESBY She's pretty important, yeah?

SERAFINA Are you sure she's asleep?

LEE SCORESBY Sure is.

SERAFINA Then I can tell you that she's more important than you can imagine. We witches fly where the veils between the worlds are thin. We hear the whispers of the immortal beings who pass from one to the other. And it's from those whispers, that we've knitted ourselves a prophecy. It's in our poems, our spells, the bedtime songs that we sing to our children. It tells of a child of destiny. A child who has it in her power to bring about the annihilation of death and the triumph of Dust.

LEE SCORESBY Are you saying that Dust is real?

SERAFINA I know it's real.

She shows him what seems to be a home-made telescope.

There was a traveller called Jopari, who came from a different world. He gave me this, my amber spyglass. See for yourself.

She hands it to him. He looks through it.

LEE SCORESBY I can't believe this. What am I looking at?

SERAFINA It's Dust, Mr Scoresby. Breathing and thinking and flowing to where it will. That is what makes our world a living place. And that's why we witches must keep Lyra safe and sound until her destiny's been fulfilled.

LEE SCORESBY So the future's fixed? She's like some clockwork doll, that you wind up and set on a path that can't be changed? Where's her free will?

SERAFINA We are all subject to the fates. But we must act as though we are not, or die of despair. And Lyra, most of all, must think her fate is malleable. If she tries to follow the prophecy blindly, she will fail. But if she acts in ignorance, out of her own true impulse, then she …

Pantalaimon appears from out of the basket, followed by Lyra, who has been listening.

LEE SCORESBY She's awake. Hi, kid.

LYRA I was fast asleep. Aren't you freezing, Serafina Pekkala?

The balloon lurches.

LYRA What's happening?

SERAFINA We're flying off course.

LEE SCORESBY Hell, we're way too high. I'm gonna release some pressure.

He pulls on a rope. Gas escapes from the balloon and it starts rapidly dropping. Roger and Iorek wake.

ROGER Help! Help!

LEE SCORESBY Nobody panic!

ROGER I'm gonna be sick!

IOREK Pull on that rope!

Lee pulls on another rope to control the descent.

LEE SCORESBY That ought to stop it.

LYRA We're still falling!

SERAFINA Look out for cliff-ghasts!

LEE SCORESBY The rope's frozen up. Give us a hammer.

Lyra helps him pull at the rope. Roger looks for a hammer.

IOREK Stand aside! I'll do it.

He goes to the rope. The basket lurches.

ROGER Please, please! Somebody stop it!

Iorek pulls at the rope and the basket lurches. A cliff-ghast climbs over the edge of the basket.

IOREK It's only a cliff-ghast.

He cuffs it and it disappears.

ROGER Look, there's another!

Another appears. Iorek lunges at it. Lee Scoresby fires and the basket rocks.

LYRA Help!

She lurches over the edge. Roger grabs her.

ROGER She's fallen out!

Lyra and Pantalaimon fall out ***into the snow.*** *Serafina and Iorek call from above:*

SERAFINA Lyra! I'll come back and find you!

IOREK Stay away from the fortress! Wait for me!

ROGER Lyra! Lyra!

On the ground, Lyra picks herself up.

LYRA Pan? Where are you?

PANTALAIMON In your bag.

He appears out of her bag as a mouse.

Are you hurt?

LYRA Dunno.

Bears appear. They circle around Lyra and sniff her with suspicion.

CHIEF BEAR Did you fall out of the balloon?

LYRA Yeah.

CHIEF BEAR Was Iorek Byrnison with you?

LYRA Er … Yeah.

CHIEF BEAR Come wi' us.

They walk on.

STUPID BEAR Where are we taking her, Sarge?

CHIEF BEAR To see the king, of course, in his marble palace.

DISGRUNTLED BEAR 'Marble palace!'

CHIEF BEAR Now, now, it isn't for us to scoff. That palace were Mrs Coulter's doing, to make us all more civilised-like.

DISGRUNTLED BEAR 'More civilised-like!'

STUPID BEAR Mrs Coulter's gonna make it so that we all get daemons, isn't she, Sarge?

CHIEF BEAR That's what she tells us, so we gotta believe it.

DISGRUNTLED BEAR Oh, it'll happen all right. Along with all the rest of her fancy notions. Reading and writing and making us cook our food. What I wouldn't give for a mouthful of raw walrus.

The bears slaver with desire at the thought of raw walrus.

CHIEF BEAR No grumbling if you please!

They arrive at the palace. Other bears are assembled there. To them:

Greetings, brothers! Find His Majesty, and humbly inform him that we've brought the prisoner.

Bears go out.

LYRA Are there other prisoners here at Svalbard? Or is it just me?

CHIEF BEAR *(to Lyra)* Do you see that window?

He points to a lit-up window very high up.

That is Lord Asriel's prison.

He moves away. Lyra looks up at the window.

LYRA It's like a star at the top of the sky. So bright an' far away. An' you just can't get to it.

She takes Pantalaimon out of her bag.

Pan, I've got an idea.

Bear-courtiers appear with Iofur Raknison at the centre. The bears pay homage to him, while Lyra slips Pantalaimon back into her bag.

BEARS Hail, King Iofur Raknison!

A bear brings Lyra forward to Iofur.

IOFUR You may kneel. Are you a spy?

LYRA No! No, I'm not!

IOFUR Then what were you doing with Iorek Byrnison? Don't deny it! You were in the balloon beside him!

LYRA I'm his daemon.

IOFUR *His daemon?*

LYRA Yes.

IOFUR Clear the court!

The other bears leave.

IOFUR If you're deceiving me, you will be fed to the starving wolves.

LYRA I know, but I'm not.

IOFUR How did that renegade outcast get a daemon?

LYRA It was an experiment at Bolvangar. There was a doctor pressed a button, and I appeared.

IOFUR *Liar!* No daemon has ever appeared in a human form!

LYRA It's 'cause … I'm an animal's daemon. Humans have animals, and animals have humans. It's like, back to front, all right?

IOFUR Then how can you travel so far away from him?

LYRA I'm like a witch's daemon. And besides … he's not very far away. He's coming to Svalbard really soon, and he's gonna raise up all the bears against you …'cause he's heard how they grumble about you.

Iofur roars.

Wait, wait, wait … And I don't want that to happen, I don't, 'cause he's a poor, sad, drunken disgrace of a bear, and you're a king with a magnificent palace. So what you gotta do … you gotta tell your guards, that when he arrives … they mustn't attack him …

IOFUR Not attack him?

LYRA … an' I'll pretend that I'm still on his side … and then you gotta challenge him in single combat! On your own! And when you've beaten him, that'll prove that you're the strongest, and then I'll belong to you! I'll be your daemon! I'll have a little throne of my own, right next to yours, and humans will come from all over the world to wonder at you! King Iofur Raknison, the bear with a daemon!

Bears enter in a state of excitement and alarm, as Iorek appears in his rusty armour.

DISGRUNTLED BEAR Iorek Byrnison is here!

BEARS Iorek is here! Iorek is here!

STUPID BEAR Shall we kill him?

IOFUR Leave him to me. Bring me my armour! I'll kill him myself!

Bears dress Iofur in armour. Lyra runs to Iorek.

LYRA Oh, Iorek, I've done a terrible thing. You've got to fight Iofur Raknison all alone, and you're hungry and tired …

IOREK How did this happen?

LYRA I tricked him! Oh, I'm sorry.

IOREK You are no longer Lyra Belacqua. Your name for ever after will be Lyra Silvertongue.

LYRA You mean I haven't done wrong?

IOREK Done wrong? To fight him is all I want!

Iofur addresses the crowd.

IOFUR Bears! Hear my command! If I kill Iorek Byrnison, his flesh will be torn apart and scattered to the cliff-ghasts. His head will be stuck on a pole above my palace gates. His name will be blotted from memory. Iorek Byrnison, I challenge you!

Iorek addresses the crowd.

IOREK Bears! If I kill Iofur Raknison, I'll be your rightful king. My first order to you, will be to tear down this palace, this perfumed house of mockery and tinsel, and hurl it into the sea. Iofur Raknison has polluted Svalbard. I shall cleanse it.

Trumpets. Iofur and Iorek square up for the fight. They prowl round, sizing each other up. They pause.

They leap together with a crash. They fight and Iorek's left forepaw seems to be wounded. Iofur taunts him.

IOFUR Whimpering cub! Prepare to die!

Iorek leaps at him: the injury was only a feint. He tears off part of Iofur's jaw and sinks his teeth in his throat. Iofur dies.

IOREK Behold! I eat the heart of the usurper!

He tears out Iofur's heart and eats it.

IOREK Now who is your king?

BEARS Iorek Byrnison!

They rush to support Iorek, who is near collapse. Roger appears.

ROGER What happened? Have I missed it?

LYRA Iorek ate the other bear's heart.

ROGER Eurgh! Yuk!

LYRA Come on, Rodge, we're going to find Lord Asriel.

*She pulls him along **through the palace and up stairs.***

ROGER The balloon crashed into a mountain. And then that goose arrived and said that one of the witches got made a prisoner at Bolvangar, so Serafina went back to rescue her. She was frightened the witch might tell them something. Then …

Thorold appears.

THOROLD Lyra! Little Lyra! Come in, child, and bring your friend with you. The Master is in his study.

He leads Lyra and Roger to a door.

LYRA ***(to Roger)*** In his *study*? I thought he was put in chains.

THOROLD You know the master. He hadn't been here a month before he'd twisted the bears around his little finger. They gave him books and instruments and a laboratory. He was both prisoner and prince.

Lyra goes into* Asriel's study*. Lord Asriel is working on a piece of scientific equipment. He looks up and sees her.

LORD ASRIEL Lyra! Get out! I did not send for you!

Lyra is dumbfounded.

LYRA What?

Roger comes in.

STELMARIA She's brought a friend.

LORD ASRIEL Who's this boy?

LYRA He's Roger. You saw him at Jordan College.

LORD ASRIEL Come here, Roger.

Roger approaches him. Lord Asriel looks at him hard. Smiles.

I'm delighted to see you. Thorold, run these children a hot bath.

ROGER Wow!

THOROLD Follow me.

Lord Asriel goes back to his work. Thorold leads Roger out. Lyra stays. Lord Asriel looks up and sees her.

LORD ASRIEL I thought you'd gone.

LYRA I'm not some bloody kid that you can have put in the bath when you feel like it. You're my father, en't you?

LORD ASRIEL Yes. So what?

LYRA So what? You should have told me before, that's what. You could've asked me to keep it secret, and I would've. I'd have been so proud that nothing would have torn it out of me. But you never.

LORD ASRIEL How did you find out?

LYRA My mother told me.

LORD ASRIEL Your mother …? Then there's nothing left to talk about. I don't intend to apologise, and I refuse to be preached at by a sanctimonious ten year-old.

LYRA I'm twelve! I'm twelve!

LORD ASRIEL Well, you would know. If you want to stay, you'd better make yourself interesting to me. Tell me about your journey here. What have you seen? What have you done?

LYRA I set you free, that's what I done. You can go.

LORD ASRIEL I'll go when I'm ready. What else?

LYRA I brought you this. The Master give it me.

She shows him the alethiometer.

I hid it and I treasured it and I kept on going, even with Tartars and Gobblers catching me, and being nearly cut away from Pantalaimon. And after all that, when I walked in the door, you looked horrified, like I was the last thing in the world you wanted to see.

LORD ASRIEL But, Lyra … you were.

LYRA Right, that's it. You're not my father. Fathers love their daughters. But you don't love me, and I love a moth-eaten old bear more than I love you. Here, take it anyway.

She gives him the alethiometer.

LORD ASRIEL I can't read this thing. It will only annoy me. Keep it.

LYRA But …

LORD ASRIEL Don't argue with me.

He gives it back to her. She's very upset.

LYRA So it was all for nothing.

LORD ASRIEL Nothing? What if I told you that you'd helped me? That in your childish innocence, you'd brought me the key to a door that had never been opened? And that behind that door, lay the greatest adventure that the human race has ever known?

LYRA I dunno what you're talkin' about.

LORD ASRIEL Well, think. You were at Jordan College. You overheard my lecture. Didn't you understand what I was saying?

LYRA Yeah, course I did! There was Dust, and that Jopari man with his hand held up like that. An' it was him what gave you the amber something? Wasn't it?

LORD ASRIEL He gave me that and a great deal more.

LYRA There was the palm trees, and the Roarer …

He laughs.

LORD ASRIEL The Roarer!

LYRA Don't laugh! I gotta find out these things. What's a … nylation?

LORD ASRIEL A nylation?

LYRA Yeah. A nylation of death. What's the Triumph of Dust? What if you're just a clockwork doll, but nobody tells you? What's Dust anyway?

LORD ASRIEL Either you've been eavesdropping more than I suspected, or you've an uncanny imagination. Dust is like a vast, invisible ocean all around us. It thinks for itself, it's conscious. And it settles on adults, never on children. It's the physical proof that something happens when innocence becomes experience.

LYRA Like how?

LORD ASRIEL Like Adam and Eve in the Garden of Eden. Do you know what original sin is?

LYRA Sort of.

LORD ASRIEL Eve fell, and the human race lost its innocence. It gained experience in return. And for the very first time, Dust entered the world. Dust loves experience. It loves what we learn, what we remember, what we make of ourselves. That's why it terrifies those poor, sad, stunted souls in Geneva. They hate the power that we have when we're truly alive. Your mother made use of that, to get the Church to pay for her experiments.

LYRA You done experiments too, though. Do you cut children?

LORD ASRIEL Oh, no. Cutting in itself is merely random cruelty. My experiment draws on something that your mother's bumbling doctors never noticed. You see, when the daemon-bond is severed … cut right through … it releases a burst of energy. Greater than any earthquake, any bomb ever made. If we could *use* that energy …

Pause.

LYRA We could travel to other worlds.

He smiles approvingly.

LORD ASRIEL Bravo.

LYRA There's millions of other worlds, en't there?

LORD ASRIEL There are as many worlds as there are possibilities. I toss a coin. It comes down heads. But in another world, it comes down tails. Every time that a choice is made, or a chance is missed, or a fork in a road is taken … a world is born for each of the other things that *might* have happened. And in those worlds they do. Somewhere out there, in one of those worlds, is the origin of all the death, the sin, the misery, the destructiveness in the world. I'm going to destroy it.

LYRA You never said nothing about any of this. Not at Jordan.

LORD ASRIEL Do you really imagine that I'd tell those scholars what I was planning? If the Church suspected, for one moment …

STELMARIA You've told her enough.

LORD ASRIEL Stelmaria is right. She's always right. Have your bath.

LYRA Can we talk in the morning? Can I ask you questions?

LORD ASRIEL Ask me whatever you like. You're my daughter. Now go.

He turns away from her. Lyra goes.

Scene 3

***Bolvangar**, partly destroyed. Serafina is there. She makes herself invisible and watches the action unseen. Mrs Coulter arrives to find Lord Boreal.*

MRS COULTER Lord Boreal? What in the world are you doing at Bolvangar? How did you get here?

LORD BOREAL I arrived by zeppelin, my dear, with a party of eminent clerics from the Consistorial Court of Discipline. They plan to conduct an interrogation, and I've been asked to help.

MRS COULTER Are you going to interrogate *me*?

LORD BOREAL Well, not today. I can't, of course, give any assurance for the future. No, you captured a witch in the course of the recent battle, and Fra Pavel believes that she holds vital information. Here she is.

Fra Pavel and other clerics bring on a witch bound to a chair. She has been tortured.

MRS COULTER Let that witch go! You haven't the right to lay one finger on her. She's the private property of the General Oblation Board!

FRA PAVEL There is no General Oblation Board. It's been closed down and its records have been expunged. Your spy-flies are decommissioned, and your bank account in Geneva was terminated at midnight.

MRS COULTER I can explain what happened.

FRA PAVEL We know what happened. The Church's entire investment in Bolvangar has been wiped out. We know that your daughter was responsible. What we do not know, and are here to find out, is what her future holds.

MRS COULTER Forgive me, Fra Pavel, this is much too subtle for me to understand. Just what are you talking about?

FRA PAVEL What do you know about the witches' prophecy?

MRS COULTER I've never heard of it. What does it say?

FRA PAVEL It states reliably, most reliably, that Lyra is either the Church's greatest friend or its darkest foe.

MRS COULTER Lyra? Lyra, my daughter? How long have you known?

FRA PAVEL Since she was born.

MRS COULTER Well, I'll do all that I can to help.

FRA PAVEL I thought you might. Where is Lyra now?

MRS COULTER She's … ah … flown to Svalbard.

FRA PAVEL Correct.

MRS COULTER May I go?

LORD BOREAL No, you may not. Fra Pavel, has this witch co-operated with your enquiries?

FRA PAVEL She's told us nothing.

He hits the witch.

LORD BOREAL Perhaps the feminine touch would be more effective. Mrs Coulter, would you be so good as to take over the questioning?

MRS COULTER Now?

LORD BOREAL Yes, now. We need her to tell us precisely what this prophecy means. Is Lyra good or evil? Should we celebrate her as our saviour, or must we hunt her down? Proceed.

Mrs Coulter takes the witch's hand.

MRS COULTER Well, witch! You heard Lord Boreal. What is the answer?

The witch shakes her head. Mrs Coulter breaks one of her fingers.

MRS COULTER *Now* will you tell us?

WITCH Never!

MRS COULTER Tell us!

She breaks another finger.

Tell us, or I will break *all* your fingers!

The witch cries.

WITCH It's in the name!

FRA PAVEL The name?

MRS COULTER What name?

WITCH Lyra Belacqua has a secret name! All that you want to know is in that name! But you will never find it out!

MRS COULTER *(to Lord Boreal)* Is there really any purpose in …

LORD BOREAL Don't stop now!

MRS COULTER What is the name? Tell us!

WITCH It is the name of one who came before. You've always feared her. Now she has come again!

FRA PAVEL Lyra's our enemy.

MRS COULTER That's not what she said.

1ST CLERIC We must fly to Svalbard.

2ND CLERIC We must capture and interrogate her.

LORD BOREAL Not yet. *(to Mrs Coulter)* Continue.

MRS COULTER Must I?

FRA PAVEL We need the name!

Mrs Coulter turns slowly to the witch.

MRS COULTER Tell us the name. Tell us the name!

She breaks another finger.

WITCH Serafina Pekkala! Let me die!

Serafina Pekkala becomes visible.

SERAFINA I am here.

She stabs the witch.

FRA PAVEL Seize her!

Serafina draws her bow and arrow. Pandemonium. Serafina escapes.

Scene 4

***The Palace at Svalbard**. Night. The bears are celebrating. Thorold appears.*

THOROLD Miss Lyra! Miss Lyra!

LYRA What's up?

THOROLD The master's packed a sledge and gone up North. And he's taken the boy.

LYRA What, taken Roger?

THOROLD Don't you remember? He said 'I did not send for *you*.'

LYRA You mean he'd sent for someone else?

THOROLD He'd sent for a child to finish his experiment. That's his way. Whatever he wants, he calls, and along it comes.

LYRA And I walked in … and he thought it was me. But he's not gonna do what I *think* he is? He *can't*.

PANTALAIMON He'll do it for sure. He wants that burst of energy.

Lyra calls.

LYRA Iorek! We gotta find Lord Asriel! *Now!*

IOREK Bears! March on to the mountains!

Lyra and Pantalaimon join the bears as they all march ***to the mountains.***

LYRA *(to Iorek)* Faster! Fast as you can!

IOREK What's that sound?

LYRA There's a zeppelin coming after us!

Fra Pavel's amplified voice is heard from the zeppelin: 'Lyra Belacqua! We can see you!'

PANTALAIMON Who is it?

LYRA It's the Church! The Church!

Machine-gun fire is heard.

IOREK Faster! We'll get ahead of them.

They reach ***a snow-bridge.***

IOREK Stop! This bridge is made of snow. It will not carry my weight.

LYRA I'll go on my own. And if ever we meet again …

IOREK … I'll fight for you as though we'd never been parted. Goodbye, Lyra Silvertongue.

LYRA Goodbye, King Iorek Byrnison.

He goes. To Pantalaimon:

Let's go.

Scene 5

They cross the bridge and reach the ***mountain top****. The Aurora appears. Lord Asriel is there beside a sledge-cum-laboratory, which includes a cage in which Roger's daemon, Salcilia, is imprisoned. Roger is tied up. Stelmaria guards him. Lord Asriel is preparing a hand-held blade. He sees Lyra.*

ROGER Lyra! He's got my daemon!

LORD ASRIEL Lyra! Get away! This is nothing to do with you.

LYRA Don't touch her! Leave her alone!

LORD ASRIEL If you distract me now, I swear I'll strike you dead.

LYRA He's my friend! Don't you care about that!

ROGER Lyra, help!

LORD ASRIEL *(to Lyra)* Stay where you are! Stelmaria!

Lyra releases Roger. Pantalaimon attacks Stelmaria. Salcilia is released and scooped up by Roger.

ROGER I've got her! I've got her!

Lyra dashes towards Roger. Pantalaimon flies to them. For a moment, Lyra, Pantalaimon, Roger and Salcilia are all together.

LYRA Roger, run!

She and Pantalaimon run. Stelmaria retrieves Salcilia and scares Roger back so he can't approach her. Lord Asriel cuts boy and daemon apart. The Aurora dips and flares. Roger rises unsteadily to his feet.

LYRA Roger! Roger, speak to me!

ROGER Feel funny.

He falls to the ground. Above them, Stelmaria is holding Roger's daemon up in triumph.

LYRA He's *killed* him!

Mrs Coulter is heard approaching.

MRS COULTER Lyra!

PANTALAIMON Quick, hide!

They do. The golden monkey bounds into view. Mrs Coulter follows.

MRS COULTER Lyra?

LORD ASRIEL Look, Stelmaria! Look!

On Lord Asriel's level, a city appears in the Aurora.

MRS COULTER Asriel!

LORD ASRIEL Look at that pathway! Look at the sun … it's the light of another world! Don't turn your back on it, Marisa.

She approaches him.

MRS COULTER Was Lyra here? Did you cut her? Tell me!

LORD ASRIEL I cut the boy. And it worked! Look at the Dust that's bathing us both in glory. Feel the wind … let it blow on your hair, your skin …

Their daemons move closer together. Lord Asriel and Mrs Coulter kiss.

MRS COULTER Let me go!

LORD ASRIEL I'll tell you a secret. Nobody knows but you. I'll go through to that world, then into another, on and on, until I've found the Authority. Then I'll destroy him.

MRS COULTER You're insane.

LORD ASRIEL Come with me, Marisa. We'll work together. We'll smash the universe into pieces, and put it together in a new way. Isn't that what you want? To be part of my plan?

MRS COULTER I can't. I have to stay in this world and find our daughter. She's in danger from the Church.

LORD ASRIEL And you'll protect her?

He laughs.

You of all people? You lied to her. You tried to corrupt her. You put her father in prison. If I were her, I'd run from you as fast as my legs would take me, and I'd keep on running.

The zeppelin is heard: 'Lyra Belacqua! Give yourself up! Walk into an open space and raise your hands.'

MRS COULTER *Now* do you believe me?

LORD ASRIEL Why do they want her?

MRS COULTER What have you done to deserve to know? Go to your Dust, your filth.

LORD ASRIEL Go to your dreary, sad little machinations.

Their daemons move apart. Mrs Coulter calls.

MRS COULTER Lyra? Lyra, are you here?

She walks away and out of sight.

LORD ASRIEL I don't need you!

Lord Asriel and his daemon walk into the Aurora.

LYRA What do we do? We can't go back.

PANTALAIMON We gotta go forward, then. To where the Dust is.

LYRA I'm frightened, Pan.

PANTALAIMON Me too. But if your mother, and all those other wicked people think that Dust is bad, it's probably good. And don't you remember what Lord Asriel said?

LYRA It's 'heads in one world, tails in another …?'

PANTALAIMON Roger's dead in this world … but there could be another world where he's still alive. And we promised to find him.

LYRA Come on.

She and Pantalaimon climb up, walk into the Aurora and go through it.

Scene 6

***Lapland.** Serafina is addressing an assembly of witches. They include Pipistrelle, Caitlin, Grimhild and Grendella. Lee Scoresby is there.*

SERAFINA Sisters, listen to me! The prophecy has begun and the child is amongst us. And now the Church is after her!

PIPISTRELLE *(and others)* Do they know her name?

WITCHES Ssh!/That name is secret!/Not in front of the stranger!

LEE SCORESBY Ladies, ladies! I'm here with the honest intention of helping you find this child.

SERAFINA Have you children of your own, Mr Scoresby?

LEE SCORESBY No. I never married, I'm childless and … well, it seems to me that this little kid had a lousy deal from her true parents, and somebody ought to make it up to her.

SERAFINA I believe you, and I'll tell you as much as any short-lived mortal is allowed to know. Lyra's secret name contains the whole of her destiny. If the Church were to find it out, they wouldn't just send a zeppelin after her. They'd set all their armies on catching and killing her. That's why we witches have to search for her through the maze of the worlds and keep her safe.

RUTA SKADI Let me speak!

SERAFINA Ruta Skadi, queen of the Latvian witches, let's hear you.

RUTA SKADI If Lyra Belacqua is truly the child of destiny, then destiny will protect her. It doesn't need us to go chasing after her.

SERAFINA So what do we do?

RUTA SKADI We fight! Lord Asriel's gone to kill the Authority. That means war, and we witches are in that war already, like it or not, because we *know our enemy*. Who hates everything that's good about human nature? Who hates the touch of flesh that we witches live by? Who cut boys and girls away from their daemons at Bolvangar, so that they'd never know the beauty of love? Who persecutes us, who tortures us? Who burns witches?

WITCHES The Church!

RUTA SKADI The Church! We've waited hundreds of years for a chance to attack it, and now that chance has come. Let's take it! Now!

SERAFINA Ruta Skadi, I hate the Church just as much as any witch here. But if we don't first make the prophecy come true, then there won't be a world for you to fight in. Lord Asriel didn't just build a pathway. He cracked the shell of the sky. Look through my amber spyglass. What do you see?

She passes the amber spyglass to Grendella, who looks through it.

GRENDELLA Dust is flowing away.

There's a general gasp of worry and alarm. Grendella passes on the amber spyglass and more witches look through it.

SERAFINA All across the North, raggedy doors and windows have opened that were never there before. Dust is falling through them into a void, an absence, and so it will go on, worse and worse, till nothing is left, not a breath, not a gasp, unless the child of the prophecy, true to her secret name, brings not the defeat of Dust, not the loss of the loveliest gift of the stars, but its joyful return.

That's why we must guard and protect her, till the prophecy has run its course.

PIPISTRELLE How can this short-life help us?

WITCHES Tell us!/How?

LEE SCORESBY I've been dreaming about a man who I fought beside one time. He was a soldier from another world. But when I see him in my dream, he's changed, he's like some tribal medicine man. He knows where Lyra's run away to. And I've seen where he's hiding out, I dreamed it like I was seeing it on a map. I can lead you to him in my balloon. He'll take you to Lyra.

RUTA SKADI What's his name?

LEE SCORESBY Jopari.

A sigh of recognition from the witches.

RUTA SKADI Your dream is true. But I can't follow it.

SERAFINA Where will you go, while we fly onwards?

RUTA SKADI I'll fly to the battlefield, to fight for Lord Asriel. When you see Jopari, tell him I've not forgotten that he rejected me. I have an arrow for his heart. If I see him, I'll kill him. Farewell.

Scene 7

Cittàgazze. *Lyra and Pantalaimon come on. They have been walking for days. Lyra calls.*

LYRA Hello!

No answer.

There's nobody here either.

Pantalaimon bounds off towards a café.

Hey, where're you goin'?

PANTALAIMON It's a sandwich.

Lyra looks at it.

LYRA It's days old.

She eats a bit of salami out of the middle.

There's one good thing. We're probably safe from my mother and father.

PANTALAIMON The two most treacherous, lyingest people on all the earth.

LYRA Wasn't it awful when they kissed like that?

PANTALAIMON We made some friends, though, didn't we?

LYRA Yeah … Iorek … Serafina …

PANTALAIMON … Kaisa …

LYRA … Mr Scoresby …

PANTALAIMON … Hester …

A noise is heard in the kitchen at the back of the café.

LYRA What was that?

PANTALAIMON Let's go an' look.

LYRA We could have imagined it.

PANTALAIMON Yeah.

LYRA Nah, come on.

They walk to the kitchen and go to open the door. Will charges out and into her. They tussle. Then they pull apart and look at each other.

WILL You're just a girl.

LYRA You're just a boy. You wanna make summing of it?

WILL No! I thought that … never mind. What's your name?

LYRA Lyra Silvertongue.

WILL I'm Will. Will Parry.

She looks at him in horror.

What you lookin' at?

LYRA What 'appened?

WILL What?

LYRA Did they do it to you as well?

WILL What you talkin' about?

LYRA Your daemon! Where's your daemon?

WILL My *demon*?

LYRA Yeah. Like Pan.

WILL I haven't got a demon. I don't *want* a demon. Are you talkin' about that cat?

PANTALAIMON I think he really doesn't know.

WILL It talks!

PANTALAIMON Of course I talk. Did you think I was just a pet?

WILL That's incredible. A talking cat! Now I've seen everything. Is it … Can I pat it?

PANTALAIMON No!

LYRA Nobody pats another person's daemon. Never, ever.

WILL I was trying to be nice, that's all. Where I come from, a demon is something evil, something devilish.

LYRA Where is it? Where you come from?

WILL It … No, you wouldn't believe it.

LYRA I might.

WILL All right. I come from a different world.

LYRA You too?

WILL What do you mean, you too?

LYRA Well … So do I.

WILL Honest?

LYRA Yeah.

WILL So … how did you get here?

LYRA Through the Aurora.

WILL Rubbish!

LYRA What about you, then?

WILL I came through a window in the air. Near a bus shelter in Oxford.

LYRA That's impossible.

WILL Yeah, and walking through the Aurora, that's just normal, I suppose. Tell you what. I'll pretend to believe you, and you pretend to believe me, and then we won't have to row. All right?

LYRA Look, I don't mind.

WILL You hungry?

LYRA Yeah, a bit.

WILL There's eggs in there. I'll cook an omelette.

He goes to the fridge.

LYRA Boys can't cook.

WILL Well this boy's had to.

LYRA In my world, servants do the cooking.

WILL In my world, the coke is brown.

He produces a couple of bottles of green Coke. Gives her one.

LYRA It's cold.

WILL 'Course it's cold. Haven't you ever heard of a fridge?

He mixes eggs and makes an omelette. Two children – Angelica and her younger brother Paolo – appear.

ANGELICA Hello.

LYRA Hello.

WILL What's the name of this place?

ANGELICA Cittàgazze.

WILL Where've all the grown-ups gone?

ANGELICA They all screamed and ran away. It's nice for kids. We can go anywhere we like, and play on the pedal-boats.

PAOLO There'll be more kids coming back later.

ANGELICA We're the first.

PAOLO Along with Tullio.

ANGELICA Shut up.

LYRA Who's Tullio?

ANGELICA He's our brother, that's all.

PAOLO He's a grown-up. He's up in the tower. He's gonna …

ANGELICA Shut up, I said.

They start shouting at each other.

WILL Hold it, hold it … What did the grown-ups scream and run away from?

ANGELICA The Spectres, of course.

LYRA The *Spectres*?

ANGELICA Yeah, they're everywhere. They eat people up from the inside out.

PAOLO They suck their souls out!

ANGELICA But they don't bother kids, and kids can't see 'em.

WILL You mean, there could be a Spectre right next to us now?

The kids laugh.

PAOLO Not just one!

ANGELICA There's prob'ly hundreds!

PAOLO We're looking for ice creams. Wanna come?

LYRA No, not now.

ANGELICA Snob.

She and Paolo go.

WILL Spectres all round us.

LYRA No wonder the grown-ups ran.

WILL They ran all right.

LYRA Left their papers.

WILL Left their food.

LYRA Left their smoke-leaf.

WILL Ciggies.

BOTH What?

They look at a packet of cigarettes.

BOTH Is that what you call 'em?

Pause. They look at each other and begin to believe each other's story.

LYRA That's funny.

WILL Yeah. So what're you doing here?

LYRA I'm looking for someone. And I'm running away as well.

WILL Who from?

LYRA My mother, mostly.

WILL Fed up with you, is she?

LYRA Worse than that, 'cause I let a spy-fly loose an' I wrecked her laboratory, and I found out the Gobblers' secrets and I'm summing to do with Dust. Special Dust. Not ordinary Dust, obviously.

WILL No, obviously.

PANTALAIMON What about you?

WILL I'm running away as well.

PANTALAIMON Who from?

WILL Some people.

PANTALAIMON Bad people?

WILL Some of 'em are. *(to Lyra)* Who do I talk to? You or it?

LYRA It's 'him'. And it makes no difference. If you talk to Pan, you're talking to me in a different way.

WILL Like on the telephone?

LYRA What's a telephone?

WILL Don't you know anything?

LYRA I do! I know lots of things, but I don't know anything about your world 'cause I've never been there! That good enough for you?

She cries.

WILL I'm sorry.

LYRA It en't you. It's just everything that's been happening.

WILL I do believe you now. I'm starting to.

LYRA Me too.

WILL Let's eat.

They eat.

LYRA Except it can't be true about the window.

WILL Well, how do you think I got here? I saw the palm trees and the …

LYRA Yes, I believe the window an' the palm trees. But it can't have been in Oxford. I oughta know. I come from Oxford. Oxford's in *my* world.

WILL Then there's two different places with the same name.

LYRA Are there scholars in that Oxford?

WILL Sure are.

LYRA Is there a Jordan College?

WILL No, I don't think so.

LYRA So it's the same but different. Two Oxfords. In two different worlds.

WILL Two?

LYRA There could be more. There could be millions. 'I spread my wings, and brush ten million other worlds, and they know nothing of it.'

WILL Who said that?

LYRA A witch's daemon.

WILL Right.

LYRA A snow goose.

WILL Right, right.

LYRA You bet it's right.

WILL So … are you gonna go back? To your dusty world?

LYRA I can't, not ever. Are you gonna go back to your different Oxford?

WILL Uh huh.

LYRA What's that mean?

WILL Means I've got to, 'cause I'm looking for someone.

LYRA Will. Remember I said I was looking for someone too? Well, him an' me was best friends, and he used to live in *my* Oxford.

WILL So?

LYRA Can I come with you?

WILL Yes, if you want. Just don't come trailing around after me, that's all. You'll need some proper clothes. We'll have to borrow 'em from a shop.

LYRA What's wrong with what I got on?

WILL My world is dangerous for me. Really dangerous. An' if people notice us, they're gonna start wondering where we come from, and then they'll find the window and

I won't have this world to come an' hide in. So you gotta fit in. And don't talk to anyone. Got that?

LYRA Yeah.

WILL And wash your hair. And have a bath. If you go round smelling like that, you're really gonna stand out.

He gets up.

I cooked, so you can wash up.

LYRA I don't wash up.

WILL Then I won't show you the window. This place doesn't belong to us. So we gotta tidy up after ourselves. I'll find a bed upstairs. Goodnight.

He takes the leather writing case and goes.

LYRA That's the grumpiest boy I ever met.

PANTALAIMON Find out who he is.

LYRA I will.

She takes out the alethiometer and studies it.

PANTALAIMON What's it say?

LYRA It says he's a murderer. He's on the run from the police.

PANTALAIMON Let's go.

LYRA No, don't. It's good, in a way. It means we can trust him. And … it's moving again. It's telling me something I never even asked it.

PANTALAIMON What?

LYRA It says I gotta stop looking for Roger. I gotta stay with Will. I gotta help him find what he's lookin' for. That's my task.

Scene 8

Geneva. ***The Consistorial Court of Discipline.*** ***Mrs Coulter, Lord Boreal and Fra Pavel are there with the President. Brother Jasper sits quietly taking notes.***

PRESIDENT 'It is the name of one who came before … you have always feared her … now she has come again.' Thank you, Mrs Coulter, for having persuaded the witch to tell you.

LORD BOREAL It was a painful process.

FRA PAVEL To harden one's heart is the first step to holiness.

PRESIDENT I don't agree. As President of the Consistorial Court of Discipline, it is my task to seek out and to punish all those who would threaten the Church. The suffering that Mrs Coulter inflicted on that poor damned creature was nothing compared to the tortures that I authorise every day. But I have never once hardened my heart. I feel the lash on the heretic's back as keenly as he does. I do it to save his soul. I do it for love.

MRS COULTER My feelings exactly, Father President. As for my daughter … All I am asking for, is permission to find her. Once she's safely in my care, you can leave it to me to discover the truth about her.

FRA PAVEL Then what would be the point of the alethiometer?

MRS COULTER I've been wondering that myself. It's thrown no light on the secret name or anything else. The fact is, Father President, and I speak as a devout believer, that the Church has had chance after chance to find my daughter, and it's made a complete and utter mess of every one of them. Can you not trust her mother to track her down?

FRA PAVEL So you can do the Church's job better than it can itself?

LORD BOREAL If I may …? With all respect, at any normal time, the Church would do the job very well. But this is no normal time. Lord Asriel has broken through the Aurora into a different world and, if reports are to be believed, he plans to kill the Authority. Should we not be grateful for Mrs Coulter's help at a time like this?

FRA PAVEL Let's not exaggerate …

MRS COULTER Exaggerate!

FRA PAVEL … There was, as we all know, a similar attack on the Authority many thousands of years ago and it failed quite miserably. There's no reason to think that Lord Asriel can do any better.

LORD BOREAL There's *every* reason! That first rebellion only failed because the Authority could not be harmed by any weapon that existed at that time. But I've discovered on my travels that such a weapon has since been made.

PRESIDENT Go on.

LORD BOREAL It is a knife of astonishing sharpness. It can cut through air. It can cut through spirit with ease. It could kill the Authority. And if Lord Asriel finds it …

PRESIDENT Fra Pavel, why have I not been told about this knife? Does Lord Asriel know about it? And how can we get to it first?

FRA PAVEL I shall ask the alethiometer. But I'm afraid that three whole questions, where one alone can take up to a year to answer …

PRESIDENT I've heard enough. Lord Boreal, since it is you who has made this claim, you will find this knife, and bring it here to Geneva.

LORD BOREAL Oh, but I can't! No adult can. It's in a city thronged with Spectres who, believe it or not, devour the souls of fully grown humans. But a child could get it … a boy, a boy who can fight … a boy who can kill … and I know of exactly such a boy. His name is Will. Will Parry.

PRESIDENT Find him and send him.

MRS COULTER And my daughter, Father President?

PRESIDENT You may search for her. If you find her, you will tell us at once. There is one further matter.

He lays a hand gently on Brother Jasper's shoulder.

Am I right in believing that you can read the alethiometer?

FRA PAVEL *(who wasn't watching) Read* it? I am the world's acknowledged expert!

PRESIDENT I was speaking to Brother Jasper.

BR JASPER I read it well, Father President. I have a gift for it. I'm said to have had an angel ancestor, perhaps that's the reason.

PRESIDENT Fra Pavel, give him yours.

FRA PAVEL I beg your pardon?

PRESIDENT *(angry)* Give him yours!

Reluctantly, Fra Pavel does.

BR JASPER Where shall I start?

PRESIDENT Begin with Lyra. Ask it about the secret name. That above all is my concern. Dear friends, good day. Fra Pavel, wait in your study. You will shortly receive a visit.

Scene 9

***Cittàgazze.** Will and Lyra, looking.*

LYRA I can't see anything that even *looks* like a window.

WILL Maybe it's gone.

LYRA No, look.

The window appears. Traffic is heard.

Oh, Will! It's wonderful. Only ... what's that noise?

WILL It's the traffic on the Oxford ring road.

Lyra looks through.

Don't stand in front, or they'll see your legs.

LYRA I don't mind if they see my legs.

WILL But there won't be a body, will there? Just two legs with nothing on top, and that'll *really* freak them out. Get down and look from one side. And put that daemon of yours in your pocket.

She does.

LYRA Are you sure it's Oxford? It don't look like any bit of Oxford *I* know.

WILL Yes! Now jump through quickly and move away fast as you can.

Lyra goes through. There's the blare of a horn and a screech of brakes.

WILL Watch out!

He dashes through after her.

Are you all right?

They're in ***Will's Oxford****. We see a variety of ordinary people.*

LYRA I'm fine. I wasn't expecting it all to be so busy.

WILL This isn't busy. It's just people and cars. Let's move on, there's someone looking.

They do.

LYRA Maybe I better stick with you for a bit.

WILL Well, just don't talk to anyone. Not one word. You got that?

LYRA Yeah, all right.

She stares around in amazement.

All these people, and not one of 'em's got a daemon!

WILL Stop staring.

They walk on.

LYRA What's them white dots on the pavement?

WILL Chewing gum. Don't ask.

She approaches someone waiting at the bus shelter.

LYRA Excuse me. Is this the way to the centre of town?

Will pulls Lyra away.

WILL *Never* do that again.

LYRA What you talking about?

WILL You were calling attention to yourself. You gotta keep quiet and still, then people won't notice you. Look, just believe me, Lyra, I've been doing it all my life. You're not being serious.

LYRA Serious? I'm the best liar there ever was. I lie and shout and make a big show, and I sort of … hide behind it. And I don't get caught, not ever. You're the one who's not being serious. You're meant to be hiding from the police, and you en't got the first idea.

WILL Who said I'm hiding from the police?

LYRA You are, though, aren't you? 'Cause you murdered someone.

WILL Let's go in here where it's not so busy.

*The **Botanic Gardens.** The tree and bench are there.*

LYRA Will! It's the Botanic Gardens. We got one in my Oxford too, just the same. *Exactly* the same.

WILL Sit down.

Lyra does.

How did you know about me?

LYRA I asked this.

She produces the alethiometer.

It's an alethiometer. I ask it whatever I want to know, and it tells me.

WILL You were spying on me!

LYRA I wasn't! Well, not much. 'Cause then it told me to forget everything what I was plannin' to do, and help you instead. And I hate that. It makes me really angry. But it's what it said, an' I can't say no, so what're you lookin' for? Tell me.

WILL I'm looking for my father. He went to the Arctic on an expedition when I was still a baby, and he vanished. His name was John, John Parry. A soldier. And when I got older … these men started hanging about the house, and telephoning my mum. She said they were spooks … like … secret service people.

LYRA What did they want?

WILL This.

He shows her the green leather writing case. Opens it.

It's got my father's letters inside, that he wrote from the Arctic. The spooks kept on hassling us to get them, and my mother got ill, so I took her to stay with a friend. And that same night, I woke up to hear two men inside the house. Rummaging round and whispering. I hid behind a door at the top of the stairs … and one of them came up, very slowly, an' he stopped … an' I ran out and crashed into him. Hilarious really, a kid like me attacking a trained killer. Except that Moxie, my cat, was just behind him. Here.

He gestures to the back of his knees.

And he tipped right over her and crashed down the stairs. And he was dead. I grabbed this case and ran, an' that's when I came to Oxford. 'Cause there's books here, and libraries and newspaper offices. And I can find out all about my father. This is the last letter he wrote. He's up in the Arctic, and he's found an 'anomaly'. Something peculiar. He's put the directions down, longitude, latitude, everything. It's at a place called Lookout Ridge, and there's a rock that's shaped like an eagle.

LYRA An' what's the anom … the anomaly?

WILL That's what I wanna find out.

LYRA I'll help you, Will.

WILL You can if you like, but I don't want you using that machine of yours. It's like finding out secrets about me. Things I don't tell anyone.

LYRA All right, I won't.

WILL Why should I trust you?

LYRA I told you about my friend Roger. Only I didn't tell you everything. I thought I was saving his life, and instead I took him to the most dangerous place he could have been. And now he's dead. I'll never betray a friend again, I promise.

She gives him the alethiometer in its bag.

Take this. Just for today. It's the most precious thing I got. It means that I trust *you*.

He takes it.

WILL And you take this.

He gives her the writing case.

I'll meet you back here.

Scene 10

Will's Oxford. Lord Boreal approaches the desk of a ***cuttings library****. The librarian is there, with an assistant. Will is at a table, keeping tight hold of the alethiometer bag. He reads and makes notes.*

LORD BOREAL Good morning.

LIBRARIAN Good morning, sir. We haven't seen you in the library for quite some weeks.

LORD BOREAL I've been away. I sent a message about some cuttings I wish to read.

ASSISTANT *(to the librarian)* I'm looking them up right now, sir.

LORD BOREAL Only now? I did explain that it was urgent.

ASSISTANT Was it 'P. A. double-R. Y.', sir?

LORD BOREAL 'Parry', that is correct. Major John Parry.

ASSISTANT That's odd. One of the files is out already. It must be with that young lad over there. He said he was doing some research for a school project.

LIBRARIAN Well, get it off him!

Lord Boreal sees Will.

LORD BOREAL Please … do no such thing. I'd hate to think that I was stunting his education. And bring me the rest.

He approaches Will.

Would you mind if I shared your table?

Will nods while trying to look unnoticeable.

I do admire you young people. You know exactly the information that you want, and where to find it. May I?

He takes a cutting and reads from it.

'ARCHAEOLOGICAL EXPEDITION VANISHES.' This was the Nuniatak dig, was it not? I remember it well. There were scientists, geologists and a military adviser.

But of course you'd know that.

Slowly, Will turns to face him.

WILL Why?

LORD BOREAL Because the military adviser was your father. I had a shrewd suspicion that you'd want to read about his adventures. But I didn't expect to find you quite so soon.

Will glances at the door in panic.

Don't be afraid. I won't give you away unless you force me to.

The assistant approaches.

Are those for me?

ASSISTANT That's right, sir. The lad's not bothering you, I hope?

LORD BOREAL Not at all! We're getting acquainted, aren't we, Will?

The assistant moves away.

Oh yes, I know your name. I know your face, from the records that my friends in the secret services have been keeping on you. I know why you're on the run. I knew the man you killed.

WILL What do you want?

LORD BOREAL Lower your voice, and listen carefully. I need to send you on an errand. It's a difficult one and it may require you to kill again. I strongly advise you to do as I say. Or would you rather I had you arrested?

WILL You won't, though, will you? 'Cause if I was arrested, I wouldn't be any use to you. So sod off.

Lord Boreal smiles.

LORD BOREAL That's a very good answer. Do get in touch, if you change your mind. I'll leave my card.

He does.

Oh, by the way. There's something here that I think might interest you.

'LEGENDS OF THE ARCTIC by Major John Parry.' He produces a cutting from his wallet and reads.

WILL Give it to me!

LORD BOREAL Don't be impatient, Will.

He skims on.

... yes, here we are. 'In a place unknown, near a rock in the shape of an eagle, is a strange anomaly: a doorway into the spirit-world. Only the bravest warriors dared to enter. None had returned.'

He gives Will the cutting.

'None had returned.' Good day.

Will reads the cutting with single-minded interest. Lord Boreal takes the alethiometer-bag and leaves. Will turns and sees that the bag has gone. He springs up.

WILL Stop him! Stop that man!

He runs out.

Scene 11

***Cittàgazze**. In the mountains. Jopari is tracing a large circle with his staff. He is ill but mentally vigorous. Lee Scoresby is there. Jopari calls upwards.*

JOPARI Witches! Come down to rest for a moment.

He sits exhausted. The witches descend to earth. Meanwhile:

LEE SCORESBY Is this the world that the little gal came to?

JOPARI It is. And it's the world that I first arrived in when I left my home. I was looking for a window in the air, like the one that we've just flown through. But the snow was so thick, and the blizzard so blinding, that I walked right through it without even knowing it was there. I never found it again. So I made a new life for myself, of a different kind.

To the witches:

Welcome to Cittàgazze!

CAITLIN We can breathe.

GRIMHILD But the air feels different.

PIPISTRELLE When we flew through the clouds, even the rain felt different on our faces.

JOPARI Stay in the circle! You'll be safe inside it for a moment or two until the charm wears off. After that you'll be food for the Spectres, just like any short-lived mortal.

He points:

Do you see them now? Drifting, shimmering, like smoke in a mirror. They've multiplied like flies since I saw them last. You must go. Good luck to you all, as you search for your child of destiny. Serafina, you will not see me again. I am dying. Farewell.

SERAFINA Farewell.

The witches go.

LEE SCORESBY It's a dangerous world those gals have come to.

JOPARI They'll be safe enough as long as they keep to the air. And so shall I. That's why I called you, Mr Scoresby.

LEE SCORESBY You called me nowhere, you old witch doctor. I came to you of my own free will.

JOPARI You came to me because of a dream. I sent you that dream. I needed you and your power of flight to take me further on, to a city beside the sea.

LEE SCORESBY I never signed up to be no cab driver!

JOPARI This is important. In a tower they call the Tower of Angels, there's a man named Giacomo Paradisi. He's old and frail, but when he was young he fought for a knife, and won it. Now he must take that knife on a long and perilous journey. I must give him that order before I die. And you must take me to him in your balloon.

LEE SCORESBY Will it be good for Lyra?

JOPARI It will be good.

LEE SCORESBY Then let's hit the trail.

Scene 12

***Will's Oxford.** Lyra and Will are there.*

LYRA How could you let him *steal* it? I can't do *nothing* without it. Nothing! I can't find Roger. I can't know nothing about what my mother's up to …

WILL Look, I said I was sorry. He distracted me. He showed me something that my father had written.

He stops.

LYRA *What?*

WILL I've just remembered something. He left his card. I've got his address.

He takes out Lord Boreal's visiting card.

Sir Charles Latrom, Limefield House, Headington, Oxford.

LYRA Good. Let's burgle him.

WILL We can't.

LYRA Iorek Byrnison would.

WILL Yeah, I would too, if I was a ten-foot bear. Lyra, there'll be wires and alarms and lights flashing all over the place.

LYRA So what we gonna do?

WILL We'll go and see him.

*They have arrived at **Lord Boreal's front door.** Will and Lyra knock on the door. Lord Boreal appears.*

LORD BOREAL Will Parry? I've been expecting you.

Lyra and Lord Boreal recognise each other.

And Lyra Belacqua! This is a surprise!

LYRA Lord Boreal! How did you get here?

LORD BOREAL Did you really suppose that you were the only person to travel between the worlds? I've been coming to this one very much longer than you. 'Latrom', of course, is a name that I chose for my private amusement. Shall we talk business?

WILL There's nothing to talk about. You stole something that belongs to Lyra, and we want it back.

LORD BOREAL Is it this?

He takes the alethiometer out of his pocket.

LYRA Give it to me!

LORD BOREAL Oh no, not yet. I had assumed, Master Parry, that the bag you were clutching in the reading room was the case of letters that my friends in the secret services here are so anxious to find. Instead, I discovered this curious object. It would sit very nicely in my collection of antique instruments … but its value for me is reckoned entirely in the heartbroken look on Lyra's face as I hold it in front of her. I have a bargaining chip.

WILL Give it back to us.

LORD BOREAL I'll happily do so, but on one condition. You see, there's something else that I want much more.

LYRA Get it yourself!

LORD BOREAL I can't. It's in a place where only children can survive. Lyra, I know you've been there. Go back, and look for a tower with stone angels carved around the doorway. In that tower, there is a knife. I must have that knife. Master Parry, you'll need to fight the Bearer to get it off him. But he's an elderly man, he'll be no match for a hardened murderer like yourself. Bring me that knife and Lyra will get her toy back. Return without it, and I shall call the police. Now off you go.

Will and Lyra leave.

Scene 13

Cittàgazze: ***The Torre degli Angeli.*** *Lyra, Will and Pantalaimon look at it. An old man – Giacomo Paradisi – is at the top of the tower, fighting over a knife with an agile young man: this is Tullio. Paradisi is bloodied and wounded. Tullio grabs the knife off Paradisi and disappears to descend down the interior of the tower.*

PARADISI You down there! Run! Run! He's taken the knife!

Will moves to get away.

WILL Let's go.

LYRA Where're you goin'? You gotta stay an' fight.

WILL You serious?

LYRA 'Course I'm serious! It was you that lost the alethiometer, so you gotta get it back.

WILL But he's got the knife an' I've got nothing.

Tullio rushes out of the door. He sees Will and threatens him with the knife.

LYRA If you don't, I will!

She rushes at Tullio.

TULLIO Get away! I'll kill you!

Will pulls Lyra away and turns to face Tullio. They fight. At first, Will fares badly. Then he starts to fight dirtily and with determination, and wins possession of the knife. Tullio looks around in terror.

TULLIO Give it back! Please! You don't need it! You're just a kid!

LYRA Come on!

She drags Will into the tower, and they climb the stairs unseen. Tullio sees the Spectres approaching him. He waves his arms in the air, as though fending off a cloud of bats. He turns to the wall of the tower and inspects it closely. Finally he stands frozen and immobile. Lyra and Will appear on the roof of the tower.

LYRA Was that the bearer?

PARADISI No, I am the Bearer. He stole the knife from me and, like a fool, he thought that he could use it.

He takes the knife and calls down to Tullio:

Only the Bearer can use it!

LYRA Will! Your fingers! He's cut off your fingers!

Will looks at his hand. His little finger and the one next to it have been cut off. Paradisi sees this.

PARADISI You've won the knife. When I was a boy, I fought and won it, just like you. You see?

He shows his hand, from which two fingers have been severed like Will's.

These missing fingers are the badge of the Bearer. Now it has passed to you.

He offers Will the knife.

WILL Look, the only reason I got mixed up in this is because of a man who wants the knife for himself.

PARADISI I know the man you mean. Don't give him the knife. He will betray you. Take it.

WILL No!

PARADISI With this knife, you can cut windows between the worlds.

For the first time, Will wants the knife.

Take it.

Will takes the knife.

PARADISI Its name is 'Æsahættr'. Hold it ahead of you.

Will holds out the knife.

Now feel. You're looking for a snag, a gap so small you'd never see it, but the tip will find it, if you put your mind there.

WILL I'm feeling sick.

PARADISI Relax. Don't force it. The knife is subtle. Place your mind where the edge is sharpest. *Be* the tip of the knife.

WILL I can feel … the snag.

PARADISI Now think of nothing else. If for a single moment your thoughts should waver, the knife will break. Tease the point into the heart of the snag … and cut.

Will cuts. A window opens. Traffic is heard.

LYRA It's Oxford.

PARADISI Now you must learn to close the window. That's my last lesson. Then I shall wait on this roof top, out of the Spectres' range, until I die.

He shows Will, using his fingertips.

Feel for the edge, just as you felt with the knife. Put your whole soul into the tips of your fingers. Then … pinch it.

Will tries. Lyra and Paradisi watch. The traffic noise continues.

WILL I can't. Just can't.

LYRA You're trying to shut out the pain. You gotta accept it.

WILL All right, I'll try.

He tries, and pinches the window closed. The traffic noise stops.

PARADISI Now you are the Bearer. You can slice the air and heal it. You can travel between the worlds. You can prevail against men, monsters, spirits, spectres, even the most high angels. And in the war that is to come, you may be called to aim it even higher.

Closing montage: Serafina and the witches appear in the sky.

SERAFINA Look, sisters! Angels!

She looks through her amber spyglass.

Angels whirling and swooping in battalions, just as they did all those aeons ago when they made war on the Authority and were defeated.

GRENDELLA There was no Lyra then, and no Lord Asriel.

SERAFINA You think it's possible, then, that they could win this time?

WITCHES Yes!/The Church will fall!/The Authority will die!/Dust will triumph!/Fly on!/Fly on to Lyra!

*

Lord Asriel appears in his fortress.

LORD ASRIEL Into this wild abyss the wary fiend
Stood on the brink of Hell and looked a while
Pondering his voyage.

Mrs Coulter appears with the golden monkey.

*

MRS COULTER Lyra, where are you?

*

On the tower:

WILL Father! I'm coming to find you!

*

The President appears. Brother Jasper meets him:

BR JASPER Father President.

PRESIDENT Well?

BR JASPER I have discovered Lyra Belacqua's secret name.

He hands the President a sheet of paper. The President reads it.

Will, Lyra and her daemon Pantalaimon

Lord Boreal, Mrs Coulter and her daemon the Golden Monkey

Lyra, Will and the boatman

Will, Serafina and Lyra

Lyra, Will, Iorek and the knife

Lord Asriel and his daemon Stelmaria

Cast List

Part 2

Lyra Belacqua
Pantalaimon, *her daemon*
Will Parry

GENEVA
President of the Consistorial Court
Brother Jasper
Hardball Cleric
Softball Cleric
Fervent Cleric
Wily Cleric

OXFORD
Lord Boreal
Mrs Coulter
The Golden Monkey, *her daemon*

CITAGAZZE
Serafina Pekkala, *Queen of the Lapland witches*

Kaisa, *her daemon*
Pipistrelle
Caitlin
Grimhild
Grendella
Giacomo Paradisi
Angelica
Paolo

LORD ASRIEL'S FORTRESS
Lord Asriel
Stelmaria, *his daemon*
Lord Roke, *a Gallivespian*
The Chevalier Tialys, *a Gallivespian*
Lady Salmakia, *a Gallivespian*

CITAGAZZE MOUNTAINS
Ruta Skadi, *Queen of the Latvian Witches*
Jopari, *a Shaman*
Balthamos, *an angel*
Baruch, *an angel*

NORTHERN MOUNTAINS
Iorek Byrnison, *an armoured bear*

OUTSIDE THE LAND OF THE DEAD
Perkins, *an official*
Jeptha Jones
Hanna, *his wife*
Old Mother Jones' Death
Lyra's Death
Boatman

LAND OF THE DEAD
No-Name, *a harpy*
Harpies

Roger Parslow

UNKNOWN WORLD
Kirjava, *Will's daemon*

Scholars, students, stolen children, party guests, Trollesunders, witches, clerics, bears, cliff-ghasts, ghosts, Tartar guards and others.

Part 2

Act One

Scene 1

Opening montage:

Lyra and Pantalaimon are running.

LYRA Run, Pan! Run!

*

Lord Asriel and Mrs Coulter are there.

LORD ASRIEL Look at that pathway! Look at the sun … it's the light of another world! Don't turn your back on it, Marisa. Come with me. We'll smash the universe into pieces, and put it together in a new way. Isn't that what you want? To be part of my plan?

Mrs Coulter pulls away from him.

MRS COULTER I can't.

*

Roger is dying.

ROGER Feel funny.

Lyra embraces him.

LYRA Roger! Rodge!

*

Serafina addresses the witches.

SERAFINA Sisters, listen to me! The prophecy has begun, and the child is amongst us. And now the Church is after her …!

WITCHES Do they know her name?

SERAFINA Not yet! That's still our secret. And now we must find her and keep her from harm until her destiny's run its course.

*

Lyra meets Will.

LYRA Where is it? Where you come from?

WILL No, you wouldn't believe it.

LYRA I might.

WILL All right. I come from a different world.

LYRA Well … So do I.

*

Mrs Coulter is putting her case to the President.

MRS COULTER All I am asking for, Father President, is permission to find my daughter. Once she's safely in my care, you can leave it to me to discover the truth about her.

PRESIDENT You may search for her. But if you find her, you must tell us at once.

MRS COULTER Of course!

*

Will and Lyra are together.

WILL I'm looking for my father. He went to the Arctic on an expedition when I was still a baby, and he vanished. His name was John, John Parry.

*

Jopari appears with Lee Scoresby.

JOPARI In that tower is a man named Giacomo Paradisi. He's old and frail, but when he was young, he fought for the knife and won it. Now he must take that knife on a long and perilous journey.

LEE SCORESBY Will it be good for Lyra?

JOPARI It will be good.

*

Lyra watches as Will and Tullio fight. Will wins.

LYRA Will! Your hand!

*

Ruta Skadi confronts Serafina Pekkala.

SERAFINA So where will you go, while we fly onwards?

RUTA SKADI I'll fly to the battlefield, to fight for Lord Asriel. When you see Jopari, tell him I've not forgotten that he rejected me. If I see him, I'll kill him.

Scene 2

Brother Jasper approaches the President.

BR JASPER Father President.

PRESIDENT Well?

BR JASPER I have discovered Lyra Belacqua's secret name.

He hands the President a document. The President reads it.

PRESIDENT Summon the Council!

Bells toll. Church dignitaries assemble in ***the Consistorial Court of Discipline.*** *Brother Jasper is there. The President addresses the conclave.*

PRESIDENT Princes of the Church, we face the gravest possible crisis. Brother Jasper, our new alethiometer reader, will tell you what he has learned. You will debate it and determine what should be done. I shall not speak.

He motions to Brother Jasper, who takes the floor.

BR JASPER Ever since Lyra Belacqua was born, it has been known that she's the child in the witches' prophecy, the child who will either redeem the Church or bring about the triumph of Dust, one or the other. The answer to this riddle could be found only in a secret name … and which the alethiometer has now revealed. That name is Eve, the fount of original sin and the cause of Dust's invasion of the world. The Triumph of Dust!

HARDBALL CLERIC Father President, this is *not* the major crisis.

SOFTBALL CLERIC I agree.

HARDBALL CLERIC Brother Jasper here has raised a problem, which *may* affect us at some time in the future. What's happening *now*, is that Lord Asriel is planning to kill the Authority. *That's* what we have to deal with.

FERVENT CLERIC So Dust takes over the world while we ignore it?

HARDBALL CLERIC I'm not convinced that it will.

SOFTBALL CLERIC I'm not convinced that Brother Jasper has read the alethiometer correctly. I think he's young and over-enthusiastic and he's got carried away. I also feel that this obsession with children and Dust is taking us back to the worst excesses of the General Oblation Board!

HARDBALL CLERIC How do we know that this so-called prophecy isn't just some superstitious twaddle dreamed up by the witches?

FERVENT CLERIC Disgraceful!

WILY CLERIC Speaking on behalf of the Society of the Holy Spirit, I think it might help if we knew what Lord Asriel was actually doing.

The hardball cleric sighs with impatience.

HARDBALL CLERIC I'll spell it out. He is building a fortress. He is constructing weapons of awesome potential. He's issued a rallying call to malcontents throughout the universe, angels included.

WILY CLERIC But will the angels join him?

HARDBALL CLERIC They certainly will. They're still smarting from the last rebellion.

FERVENT CLERIC They're smarting because they were soundly thrashed! And their leader was cast into eternal perdition, and *that* will be Lord Asriel's fate, you mark my words!

HARDBALL CLERIC	But there's a knife this time. The subtle knife. 'Æsahættr.' It can kill the Authority just as surely as though he was a human being. I propose that we attack Lord Asriel *now*, before he gets it.
SOFTBALL CLERIC	But I wonder … is it quite wise to rush into a war, before we know who's got the ultimate weapon? What if we find ourselves on the losing side?
FERVENT CLERIC	Are you suggesting that the Authority could be defeated?
SOFTBALL CLERIC	If Lord Asriel gets the knife then, yes, he very well could.
WILY CLERIC	I must point out that we don't yet know if the Authority really needs our help. He hasn't asked for it.
SOFTBALL CLERIC	He hasn't talked to anyone since … would it be Saint Teresa?
WILY CLERIC	Teresa the seventh. My point is this. When war breaks out, it will be angels fighting angels in the heights of Heaven. And heavenly matters aren't our first concern. We guard the Church on Earth. We guard its borders, we guard its power, we guard its wealth. And it's our duty, it seems to me, to have the wherewithal to do just that, and nothing more.
FERVENT CLERIC	Are you seriously saying that we ought to wait till we see who's got the knife, before we decide what side we're on?
SOFTBALL CLERIC	No, that's what *I* was saying. What his reverence here is saying, is that we should

60

65

70

75

80

85

get the knife for ourselves, and then hang on to it.

FERVENT CLERIC Saints preserve us!

WILY CLERIC Well, it would guarantee the Church's power for a thousand years. What would be wrong with that?

SOFTBALL CLERIC It might look opportunistic.

WILY CLERIC How it would *look*, of course, is very important. Our brethren in the colonies would be very upset indeed if they thought we were cooking up some kind of compromise.

FERVENT CLERIC And rightly so!

PRESIDENT You are all dismissed!

They file out. As they go:

HARDBALL CLERIC That went very well. We'll be at war before we know it.

WILY CLERIC I think we may.

They have gone.

PRESIDENT *(to Brother Jasper)* They understand nothing of Dust. Nothing of Eve. Nothing of what must be done. Come closer.

Brother Jasper does.

Find out where Lyra is hiding.

BR JASPER And then?

PRESIDENT I want you to gather a band of warriors. Young men like you, pure in heart and ready to die for the sacred cause. Young men who can kill. They will receive their orders later. Go in peace.

Scene 3

The air over Cittàgazze. *The witches are flying.*

SERAFINA Fly on, sisters!

PIPISTRELLE I've seen no sign of the child.

WITCHES Nor me!/Nor me!

SERAFINA But she's here in Cittàgazze. That we know. Jopari told us. Fly on!

WITCHES Fly on! Fly on!

Scene 4

Oxford. Night. Will and Lyra at the ***iron gate to Lord Boreal's house.*** *It's locked shut. Lyra rattles the gate.*

LYRA What do you think?

WILL Let's try.

He uses the knife to cut through the gate, and they go through.

LYRA Look, there's the house, and there en't any lights on, so he's gotta be out.

WILL Hang on.

LYRA Is your hand still hurting?

WILL Yes, and it's bleeding like anything. Do up the bandage, will you?

She starts doing so.

LYRA I did this.

WILL Yeah, well shut up about it.

LYRA I did. You'd never have fought that man if I hadn't pushed you into it. 'Cause I wanted the alethiometer back, and I shouldn't've done. I'm meant to be helping you find your dad.

WILL Well, you forgot for a minute. Let's get on with what we're doing.

LYRA We don't have to. We could knock on Lord Boreal's door and give him the knife, like we said we was going to.

WILL Then he'll have *both* our things. Look, it's all decided. We'll keep the knife, and burgle his house and take back the alethiometer.

LYRA How?

WILL You stay here. Then I'll cut a window from this world into Cittàgazze, and I'll walk to where I think his study is, cut into it and grab the alethiometer, then I'll jump back into Cittàgazze-world, run back here, you come through, and I'll close up the window. Got it?

LYRA You're gonna cut into another world, walk along a bit and cut back into this one?

WILL Yeah.

LYRA While I stay here?

WILL That's it. Don't bother me now. If I think about anything else, the knife's gonna break, remember? And, Pan, you better do your mouse act again.

PANTALAIMON I was expecting that.

He turns into a mouse.

WILL Take this.

He gives Lyra the green leather writing case and cuts a window.

I won't be a minute.

He goes through. Mrs Coulter is heard approaching.

MRS COULTER Is it through this gate?

LYRA Will!

Lyra goes through the window after him. Lord Boreal and Mrs Coulter appear.

MRS COULTER So this is your secret world! It's charming, Charles.

LORD BOREAL I hardly believe its charm is what made you insist that I brought you here.

MRS COULTER Of course it isn't. I want my daughter. Will I be sharing a room with her?

LORD BOREAL No, certainly not. I've asked my manservant to make up the guest room for you.

MRS COULTER The guest room? Well, we mustn't upset him. I must remember to rumple the sheets in the morning. You really are the most delightfully old-fashioned host.

They have reached the front door.

LORD BOREAL After you.

They go into the house. Will appears, peering

down through a knife-made window in the ceiling of Lord Boreal's study. Lyra appears.

LYRA Will!

WILL What are you doing? I told you to stay outside.

LYRA He's back, and he's brought my mum! If she finds me, I'm done for!

She sees the window.

Where are we anyway? Why's the window pointing downwards?

WILL It's the only way I could cut in. The ground level here must be lower or something.

LYRA Yeah, that's right … 'cause it's a different world, so the hills and valleys can all be different too.

WILL Let's hope they don't look up at the ceiling.

LYRA Well, at least we en't poking up through the floor.

Lord Boreal is heard outside the study.

LORD BOREAL Leave your bags in the room on the left.

WILL Ssh!

Lord Boreal comes into the study. He puts away the alethiometer.

LYRA He's got the alethiometer!

Lord Boreal opens a drawer, takes out a revolver, checks it and puts it back.

Look!

The golden monkey bounds in, followed by Mrs Coulter.

MRS COULTER And just what do you do in this world, exactly?

LORD BOREAL Very much as I do at home. I raise prize orchids, I collect antiques and I have a not-too-stressful posting with the secret services. May I offer you a glass of sherry?

MRS COULTER Thank you.

He pours sherry. Meanwhile:

Now you are quite certain that Lyra's coming?

LORD BOREAL Without a doubt. She wants her pretty piece of clockwork.

MRS COULTER You won't *really* give it back to her, will you?

LORD BOREAL Oh, no. Although I'm sure she'll scream and shout and cause an appalling scene.

MRS COULTER She'll learn to behave when I've got her under lock and key, I can assure you of that.

LYRA *(to Will)* Bloody old cow.

MRS COULTER I shall *never* forgive you for sending her into that terrible Spectre-world.

LORD BOREAL She's in no danger. Children are safer in Cittàgazze than anywhere else.

MRS COULTER Children aren't normally sent there to fight for deadly weapons. What if they both get killed?

LORD BOREAL Marisa, my dear, if there's a boy in the universe who can win that knife, it's him. Will Parry.

LYRA *(to Will)* Yeah.

Will shows Lyra his wounded hand.

WILL Yeah but.

MRS COULTER How can you be so sure?

LORD BOREAL Because he's a murderer.

MRS COULTER A *murderer*?

LORD BOREAL My dear, he's twelve years old, and he's already killed a highly trained secret service operative. Oh yes, a very bad hat. On drugs, I imagine … single mother living on state handouts …

WILL You bastard!

MRS COULTER Yes, well that's typical of Lyra. Even at Jordan, she used to find her playmates in the gutter. We had one of them at Bolvangar, a beastly little kitchen boy, called Roddy or Rudy …

LYRA I'll kill her!

WILL Calm down! I want you to go back into Oxford, come round the outside of the house and chuck a couple of stones at the window, so they go running outside, all right? I'll grab the alethiometer and run.

LYRA Yeah, all right. But I'm still gonna kill her.

She goes.

MRS COULTER But she's my daughter, Charles. And I insist on absolute frankness about your dealings with her.

LORD BOREAL Don't you trust me?

MRS COULTER No, I don't. You're keeping something back, it's obvious. Will Parry may well be a thug and hooligan, that I believe. But there are thousands of boys like that. Why was it him, and *only* him, who could get you the knife? What makes him different?

LORD BOREAL The blood in his veins.

Will climbs as far down as he can into the room to hear this.

MRS COULTER What do you mean?

LORD BOREAL Twelve years ago, Will's father, John Parry, discovered a window between the worlds. He walked through, and found himself in Cittàgazze. My friends in the secret services have been trying to find that window for years. It has profound intelligence implications …

MRS COULTER Stick to the father.

LORD BOREAL I shall. Parry is still alive, in hiding, under a different name, the name that was given to him by the Northern tribesmen.

MRS COULTER And what makes him so remarkable?

Lord Boreal is about to reply when a handful of stones clatters against a glass window.

MRS COULTER It's them, it must be!

Lord Boreal takes the revolver out of the drawer.

Charles! What are you doing?

He runs out. Will prepares to climb down into the room. Lord Boreal appears in the garden. Lyra can be seen, searching for the window into Cittàgazze. Lord Boreal calls:

LORD BOREAL Will? Will, are you there?

Mrs Coulter appears after him.

MRS COULTER Put that gun away this instant!

LORD BOREAL It's just for the boy. Only the boy.

He calls:

Don't worry, Will, I'm not going to harm you.

Mrs Coulter moves further into the garden, calling:

MRS COULTER Lyra? Lyra?

LYRA Go away!

MRS COULTER Don't be afraid, my darling! I'll look after you!

LYRA Will! Where are you?

Will appears in the Cittàgazze window, carrying the alethiometer. Lord Boreal raises his gun to fire. The golden monkey leaps at him and the gun fires into the air.

WILL Lyra! Over here!

He pulls Lyra through and closes the window. Lord Boreal and Mrs Coulter stare at the place where the window disappeared.

MRS COULTER We've got to go after them.

LORD BOREAL Marisa, we can't! They've gone into Cittàgazze!

MRS COULTER They can have gone into hell for all I care. I haven't come all this way, to be satisfied with a glimpse of my daughter by a clump of palm trees.

LORD BOREAL But the Spectres will kill us!

MRS COULTER *Will* you be quiet? You've told me about the Spectres, and … I'm sure of it … there must be a way of getting control of them. It's to do with adults and children, isn't it …? … and Dust … and everything I was working on at Bolvangar. Yes, I can do it.

LORD BOREAL Go on your own! Let me stay here!

She laughs.

MRS COULTER Have you forgotten your orders, Charles? You're getting the knife. And the knife is *there*.

She points to where the window appeared.

We'll leave in the morning.

Scene 5

***Cittàgazze.** Will lies collapsed on the ground, exhausted and in pain. Lyra is with him.*

WILL He was talking about my father. He said he found a window. Just like me. And he's *alive*.

LYRA Are you all right, Will?

WILL I'm just tired.

LYRA Ssh … Let's talk in the morning. We'll go to the place we met. I'll cook an omelette …

Will is asleep.

He's asleep.

PANTALAIMON Why do you think his father's so important?

LYRA Dunno.

PANTALAIMON Where d'you think he is?

LYRA I don't know!

PANTALAIMON You could ask the alethiometer.

LYRA Oh, Pan, you heard what he said in Oxford. I can't go snooping on him.

PANTALAIMON That makes a change. It used to be you who was always snooping, and me who tried to stop you.

LYRA I know … but I think I'm changing. Hey, Pan. If we hadn't gone snooping in the Retiring Room, do you think any of this would have happened?

PANTALAIMON Not in *this* world. But there could be another world where your father drank the poison …

LYRA … yeah … or where the gyptians never found me …

PANTALAIMON … or the Gobblers cut us apart.

LYRA … or where Roger's alive.

Serafina appears.

SERAFINA Lyra!

LYRA Serafina Pekkala! What are you doing here?

SERAFINA We've been searching for you throughout this world.

Lyra indicates to the sleeping Will.

LYRA Don't wake him!

SERAFINA Who is this boy?

LYRA It's Will. He's sick. He had two of his fingers cut off with a knife.

Serafina sees the knife.

SERAFINA That must be the reason that I could come to land. There are Spectres spread in a circle all around us, but they'll come no nearer. They fear that knife.

She walks round Will, looking at him.

He's a good-looking fellow, don't you think?

LYRA Is he?

SERAFINA There's some would think so. My sisters will be here in a trice, so tell me quickly. What is he like?

LYRA He's brave. He's good.

SERAFINA Do you trust him?

LYRA Yeah, I do … but why're you asking me all these questions?

SERAFINA It's hard for a witch to know what a short-lived girl like you might feel for a boy. We live so long, you see, for hundreds of years, never aging, never changing … and men are quite the opposite. They're like butterflies, dead by nightfall. We no sooner fall in love with them, than they're gone. We bear their children, who are witches if they are girls …

but mortals like their fathers if they are boys … and then we watch our sons growing strong and golden and handsome, knowing all the time that they'll die of old age, or on the battlefield, while we're still young, while we're still bearing son after son, each one of them just as doomed as the ones before. And finally our hearts are broken.

LYRA Was Farder Coram in love with you?

Unseen by Lyra or Serafina, Will wakes and listens.

SERAFINA He was, and I loved him. I'd fallen to earth in the Fenland marshes, where Coram was fishing, and he hauled me into his boat, or I'd have drowned. He was twenty and I was pushing two hundred … Well, I lay a week in his cabin, with the light blocked out, while I was mending from my fall. But it was summer outside, and the light was calling. One afternoon we strolled across the fields. We picked fruits from the hedgerows … we sat, we talked, we watched the river … and I lifted a blackberry and pressed it against his lips. It was only then, that I knew I loved him. Nine months later, I bore his child …

LYRA Was it a girl, a witch?

SERAFINA He was a boy, and he died very young, in the great fever. It tore a piece out of my heart, and Coram was broken by it. I would have stayed and cared for him, but I had to fly back to the North to be Queen of my clan. I hoped that he would forget me, and find a human wife.

LYRA He never did.

SERAFINA I know that now. It seems that our destinies were bound together after all, like yours and this boy's may be.

Witches appear.

WITCHES Serafina Pekkala!/We're here!/Have you found the child?

SERAFINA Not so loud. There's a young man sleeping.

The witches look at Will with great interest.

We'll guard and guide these children wherever they wish to go. So tell us, Lyra, where are you heading for?

LYRA We're looking for Will's dad. Only we don't know where to start.

KAISA May I suggest that you ask the alethiometer?

LYRA Will told me not to.

PANTALAIMON But us and him are together, aren't we? Ask it where *we* oughta go. Then it won't be snooping.

LYRA Well … just this once.

She silently asks the alethiometer.

We've got to travel to those blue mountains across the bay … and we gotta go fast. My mum's coming after me.

Scene 6

Lord Asriel's fortress. *Lord Asriel addresses his troops.*

LORD ASRIEL I stepped through the Aurora. I travelled through world after world, each one of them stranger and less familiar than the one before, until I'd found the limit that man can reach, a world beyond which lies only the spirit-domain of the Authority. And it's into this world, this final outpost of reality, that we shall tempt him. He will invade our world, and we shall fight him, just as the brightest and best beloved of all the angels fought him at the dawn of time. But with one difference. There is a knife, 'Æsahættr', celebrated in the Norsk legends, seen by Gilgamesh in a dream, foretold by the Delphic oracle to Alexander the Great. A knife so sharp, so keenly edged that it can pierce his heart as though it were human flesh. We shall have that knife. We shall defeat the Authority. We shall topple him from his throne. We shall destroy him.

Applause.

STELMARIA Fine words.

LORD ASRIEL Be quiet.

STELMARIA Why did you boast about the knife? You haven't got it.

LORD ASRIEL Jopari will bring it. He's a man of honour.

STELMARIA Jopari can't bring you anything. He's dying.

LORD ASRIEL Then how can I get it?

STELMARIA The Church has need of the knife as much as you, and they've got better intelligence. Send a spy to discover their plans.

LORD ASRIEL I'll do it.

An officer appears, very amused.

OFFICER My lord, your first recruit has arrived. But he's only that big!

He indicates minute size and the soldiers laugh. Asriel signals to them to stop.

LORD ASRIEL Bring him to me and show him the greatest respect.

The officer goes. To the others:

Lord Roke is here, the chief of the Gallivespians. I've seen him leading his men full-tilt against a Tartar battalion. He may be small, but he's a hero.

Lord Roke appears flying on a dragonfly.

LORD ROKE Hello, chaps! I wouldn't have missed this party for the world!

He lands.

LORD ASRIEL Lord Roke, what excellent timing.

LORD ROKE A stirring speech, my lord. We Gallivespians are right behind you. How can I be of service?

LORD ASRIEL Since time immemorial, Lord Roke, your countrymen have crept through keyholes, hidden in cupboards, lurked in the pockets of coats to discover the secrets that we blundering humans cannot find out.

LORD ROKE Are these kind remarks the prelude to some risky assignment?

LORD ASRIEL They are. Won't you perch on my hand?

LORD ROKE A singular honour. Pray take the greatest care to avoid my sting.

He sits on Lord Asriel's hand.

LORD ASRIEL I want you to send your two most trusted spies to the Consistorial Court of Discipline in Geneva. They will report to me daily by lodestone resonator.

LORD ROKE May I suggest the Chevalier Tialys and his spouse, the Lady Salmakia? Their sting is overwhelming, and they play very well as a team.

LORD ASRIEL Whoever you wish. I want every detail, every hint of information they can provide about the god-destroying knife. I want to know where it is kept and how the Church is planning to capture it.

LORD ROKE What a jaunt! And how they'll jump at it! I only wish it was me. I've also heard, your lordship …

He clears his throat significantly and beckons Lord Asriel closer:

… that the President of the Consistorial Court considers your daughter to be some kind of serious menace. Do you wish to know more about that?

LORD ASRIEL She's of less importance.

STELMARIA But be sure that your spies include her in their reports.

LORD ROKE Mission understood!

He salutes and flies off.

Scene 7

*Cittàgazze: **the tower**. Mrs Coulter addresses the Spectres, with the golden monkey beside her.*

MRS COULTER Spectres! Do you remember our bargain? I'll bring you human souls, and in return you'll leave us alone? Well, look what I've brought you. He's all yours! Aren't you hungry?

Lord Boreal drags Giacomo Paradisi out of the door. Both are terrified. Paradisi looks in horror as the Spectres approach him. Children, including Paolo and Angelica, appear and watch with unhealthy interest. Paradisi flails his hands in the air. Then his movements slow down and stop. He stands, lifeless and frozen. Mrs Coulter inspects him.

Total removal of the soul, just like Bolvangar. Stop whimpering, Charles! They've gone.

LORD BOREAL Never, ever, put me through anything like this again.

MRS COULTER We're in no danger! The Spectres and I have reached an understanding. As soon as you described them to me, I knew that I could dominate them, and so it turns out. Children, stay. This gentleman has a question for you.

To Lord Boreal:

Go on!

LORD BOREAL My dears, we're looking for a boy and a girl of about your age. Have you seen them?

PAOLO Yeah.

ANGELICA They're vile.

PAOLO They're evil.

LORD BOREAL Did the boy have a knife, when you saw him last?

ANGELICA Yeah, he stole it from our brother Tullio.

PAOLO Then Tullio got eaten by the Spectres, just like this old geezer.

ANGELICA Except we wasn't laughing that time.

MRS COULTER No, I'm sure you weren't. Where did they go, this boy and girl?

PAOLO Up to the mountains, there, with lots of flying ladies.

ANGELICA When you find the kids, will you kill 'em for us?

PAOLO *Please!*

MRS COULTER Carry our bags until we're out of the city, and we might consider it. And if you're really good, I'll give you a present. Do you like chocolatl?

They go.

Scene 8

Cittàgazze. ***In the mountains.*** *Evening. The witches, Lyra, Will and Pan are on trek. Will is nursing his hand. It's cold and they're all wrapped up. Serafina gives out orders.*

SERAFINA Stop! This is where we'll rest for the night. Four of you stay in the air to keep a lookout.

GRIMHILD What for?

CAITLIN The Spectres won't come near us, not while the knife's about.

SERAFINA There may be other dangers. You there, make a fire. You and you, get busy skinning our supper.

The witches get busy. Thunder. Serafina looks up at the sky.

It's going to rain.

LYRA Come on, Will. We'll all snuggle up together.

He sits with her.

WILL Here, Pan! You're getting left out.

He lifts a corner of blanket next to him for Pantalaimon, who pointedly goes the long way round to Lyra's side and gets in with her. With irony:

That's nice.

LYRA He's never gonna touch you, Will. That's one of the rules.

WILL I wish I had a daemon.

PANTALAIMON You *have*.

LYRA He's right. We're both human, en't we? It wouldn't make sense if you didn't have one.

WILL Then why can't I see it?

LYRA Not *it*. You can't see *her*, because *she* is inside you.

WILL So there's daemons in my world?

LYRA Yup.

WILL It could be true. 'Cause I think there's Spectres there as well.

LYRA What makes you think that?

WILL Well … you remember what Tullio did, when the Spectres got him?

LYRA Yeah, he got sorta interested in little tiny things, like the stones in the wall. What about it?

WILL My mum does that. I haven't told you much about her. I've not told anyone, really. She gets ill, like ill in her head, with worry and fear. She'll count the railings in the park, or the leaves on a bush or the tins in a supermarket. As though she's turning away from something that frightens her. There's plenty of real things for her to be frightened of. My father never coming back, or the men who were after his letters. But it's more than that. It's things that nobody else can see. Maybe they're the same as Spectres, only in my world we call them something else. Like mad, or looney.

LYRA Did you always want to find your dad?

WILL Yeah, always. I used to pretend he was a prisoner in a dungeon, and I'd help him escape. Or a castaway on a desert island, and I'd be the captain of the boat that rescued him. I imagined him saying, 'Well done, my son. No one on earth could have done better. I'm proud of you.' My mother used to say I was gonna wear his mantle.

LYRA What's a mantle?

WILL It's a task, a purpose. But I could never wear my father's in a million years. He was a soldier, a fighter.

LYRA You fought Tullio.

WILL I had to, didn't I? Don't think I liked it.

LYRA When I was at Jordan, I used to fight all the time, and I never been so happy in all my life. Did you not fight ever?

WILL Just once. It was one of my mum's bad times. She went out of the house not properly dressed. Well, hardly dressed. There were some boys from school got hold of her, and they tormented her. Tortured her mentally. So the next day at school, I found the boy who'd started it all. I broke his arm and I knocked out some of his teeth. Then afterwards I had to pretend I was sorry. The other kids all shut up about it. They knew that I'd kill them if they said anything that meant I got put into care, or my mum got taken away. After that, I lived a normal life. Had a couple of friends, even. But I never trusted kids again. They're just as keen as grown-ups to do bad things.

Ruta Skadi appears.

RUTA SKADI Sisters! Take cover! There's a storm approaching!

WITCHES Ruta Skadi! Welcome! Where have you been?

They welcome her to ground noisily.

RUTA SKADI I flew to Lord Asriel's fortress. Oh, if you could see it, sisters! There are great stone ramparts and battlements and towers reaching up to the stars!

WITCHES How did he build it so fast?

RUTA SKADI Who knows? I think he makes time go faster or slower however he wants. And there are fighters joining him … humans, lizards and apes, huge birds with poisonous spurs … and witches from all the worlds! *Men*-witches too!

WITCHES Never!/You're making it up!

SERAFINA Did you see Lord Asriel?

RUTA SKADI I did. I made myself invisible, and I found my way to his innermost chamber, while he was getting ready for sleep. And he asked us to join him. To fight on his side. Come with me! Fly to the battlefield!

There's a chorus of agreement from the witches.

GRENDELLA I will!

CAITLIN I'll come too!

GRIMHILD Can't we go there, Serafina Pekkala?

SERAFINA No, we can't, and you all know why! Let me talk to our sister.

Serafina and Ruta Skadi talk where they can't be overheard.

The prophecy's coming true. We've found the girl, and she's travelling with a boy.

Ruta Skadi sees Lyra and Will.

RUTA SKADI Is that him beside her? What's his name?

SERAFINA It's Will.

RUTA SKADE Come closer, Will.

Will comes nearer. He looks weaker and very ill. Ruta Skadi takes his hand and looks at him.

RUTA SKADI What's wrong with your hand?

SERAFINA It's a spirit-wound. Our spells can't heal it. The plants and herbs are all quite different in this world.

To Lyra and Will.

Go back to sleep.

They do.

RUTA SKADI I've seen those eyes before.

SERAFINA If you have, it's best for us all that you forget them.

Pipistrelle calls over, pointing upwards.

PIPISTRELLE Serafina Pekkala! There's a balloon being blown like a seabird through the skies!

Witches look up and clamour.

WITCHES Who's inside it?/Is it him?

GRIMHILD It's Jopari! It's Jopari with the Texan.

The witches check. Ruta Skadi turns furiously to Serafina.

RUTA SKADI Why did you bring Jopari into this world? Why didn't you stay in the Arctic, where you could do no harm?

SERAFINA Don't make me angry, Ruta Skadi. All I have cared about, since that child came into our lives, is that the prophecy comes true.

RUTA SKADI Then *let* it. Let it come true, or let it fail, if that's what destiny chooses. Lyra must do what she does of her own free will. Leave her alone!

Scene 9

*Cittàgazze: Mrs **Coulter's camp.** Mrs Coulter and Lord Boreal. He still has his gun. He's uneasy. She looks up and listens.*

MRS COULTER When the thunder stops, I can hear the singing of the witches. Aren't you excited?

LORD BOREAL I must confess, Marisa, that what's mostly absorbing my attention is the sight of those Spectres hovering in that copse of trees.

MRS COULTER Yes, I'll have to find someone to give them soon. It's just a shame those ghastly children weren't a little bit older. I've been thinking, Charles, what a very good team we are. You needed me to stay alive …

LORD BOREAL … and you needed me to guide you to your daughter.

MRS COULTER *(quietly to her golden monkey)* Though *that* particular task has been accomplished.

The monkey signals approval.

LORD BOREAL What did you say?

MRS COULTER Oh, nothing. What will you do, when we find the children?

LORD BOREAL I'll get the knife, and hurry back to Geneva as fast as my legs will take me. What about you?

MRS COULTER I'll keep my daughter quiet and safe.

That's all I want. When she lived with me in London, I used to sit at the end of her bed and watch her, and my heart would burst with love. Then she'd wake up and … oh … the racketing round and the noise and nuisance. I'd have to remind myself of what she was like before, and then I'd love her again. What's odd is that I still don't know the most important thing about her.

LORD BOREAL What might that be?

MRS COULTER Remember the witch I tortured? 'It is the name of one who came before …' What is that name?

LORD BOREAL I've no idea.

MRS COULTER Don't treat me like a fool. I'm sure the Church has worked it out by now. I'm certain they've told you.

LORD BOREAL Marisa, they haven't!

MRS COULTER I'm warning you, Charles! Unless you tell me *now*, you will die a revolting death. And I can do it!

She calls:

Spectres! Come closer!

Spectres approach as Lord Boreal quakes in terror. The monkey scuttles over to Mrs Coulter and hides behind her.

LORD BOREAL Marisa, I promise … I swear … I do not know that name. Don't you believe me?

She looks at him and forms a judgement.

MRS COULTER Yes, I believe you. And I'm sorry to say that it makes you utterly useless to me! Spectres! Take him!

The Spectres attack and devour him. To the golden monkey:

Let's go.

Scene 10

The witches' camp. *Moonlight. The witches are sleeping. Lyra and Will are lying on the ground. Serafina approaches.*

SERAFINA Pantalaimon!

PANTALAIMON Ssh! Lyra's asleep.

SERAFINA I must go. Ruta Skadi has left in a rage, and I'm terrified of what she might do.

KAISA Tell Will to get some sleep as well.

They go.

WILL Sleep! That's the last thing I could do. Look at my hand.

He shows his hand, which is septic and gangrenous.

It's worse than ever. I never knew anything could hurt so much. The blood's gushing out of it, and it's bad, it's smelling. Am I going to die? I'm so frightened.

Pantalaimon licks his hand.

What are you doing?

PANTALAIMON Lyra doesn't think you're frightened. She thinks you're the bravest fighter she's ever seen. She thinks you're as brave as Iorek Byrnison.

Lyra opens her eyes and listens.

WILL She's braver than me. She's the best friend I ever had.

PANTALAIMON She thinks that about you as well.

WILL What would she think of me if I died like this? In the middle of nowhere … on a stupid search for a father who went through a window and vanished …

PANTALAIMON He's still alive.

WILL He didn't bother to come home, though, did he? I've been lying here trying to think what to do. But the pain's so bad, and I get so muddled.

He stands.

I'm going for a walk.

He goes. Lyra sits up.

LYRA You touched him.

PANTALAIMON I felt sorry for him.

LYRA Shall I go after him?

PANTALAIMON No, don't. He wants to be on his own.

LYRA He said I was the best friend he ever had. What if that's the last thing I ever hear him say?

PANTALAIMON It'll be the last thing and the best.

LYRA Yeah. Yeah, you're right.

The golden monkey appears and creeps towards her. Mrs Coulter appears. Lyra sees it and springs up.

MRS COULTER Lyra! Lyra, it's me.

LYRA Go away!

MRS COULTER Don't be afraid. I'm taking you back to our own world, darling, to our beautiful world of daemons. Come to your mother.

LYRA Will! Will!

The witches awake and see Mrs Coulter.

WITCHES It's her!/The woman with the monkey daemon!/The torturing woman!

MRS COULTER Spectres! Now for the feast!

Spectres attack the witches, who shudder and struggle as their souls are devoured. Lyra screams for help. Mrs Coulter and the golden monkey carry her away.

Scene 11

Cittàgazze. ***On the mountain****. There's a rock in the shape of an eagle. Will appears, in great pain. Jopari appears out of the darkness.*

JOPARI Give me your hand.

Will stares at him.

WILL Who are you?

JOPARI It doesn't matter. Give it to me.

Cautiously, Will holds out his hand. Jopari takes out a little flask and puts ointment on it.

I came to this world to look for an old, old man. And he sent me to you … and I discover you're just a child. Well, so it must be. Don't move.

He has finished anointing Will's hand.

There.

WILL It's stopped hurting. Even the bleeding's stopped.

JOPARI Have you got the knife?

WILL What …?

JOPARI Let me see it.

WILL Here.

He gives it to Jopari, who looks at it.

JOPARI Do you know who made this?

WILL No.

JOPARI It was invented by the philosophers of Cittàgazze, three hundred years ago. They wanted to divide matter … to cut it smaller and smaller, till they'd made a particle so minute that even the strongest lens couldn't detect it … and then to divide that too. This was the result. It worked. It worked triumphantly. But they'd unleashed a power they couldn't control. The knife cut windows into other worlds, and the Spectres floated in. Here, take it.

WILL I don't want it.

JOPARI Too late. You think you chose this knife. Or that you stumbled across it. Wrong. It chose you. You are the Bearer. If you don't use it now to fight the forces of evil, it will be torn from you and used against the rest of the human race, for all eternity.

WILL Forget it, will you? I'm not gonna fight. I hate fighting.

JOPARI Did you fight to get it?

WILL Yes.

JOPARI And did you win it in single combat?

WILL Yes.

JOPARI Then you're a fighter. You're a warrior. Argue with me if you like, but don't argue against your own nature. Now listen. There are two great powers, and they've been enemies ever since time began. There's the power that wants us to obey and be humble and submit, and the power that wants us to know more, and be wiser and stronger. Every advance in human life, every scrap of knowledge and wisdom and decency has been torn by one side from the teeth of the other. Now those two powers are lining up in battle. Each of them needs that knife. You have to choose. We've both been guided to this place, this night, this moment … you with the knife, and me to tell you what you must do with it.

WILL You're wrong! I know what I'm doing. I'm searching, right? And it's not for the knife. It's …

JOPARI Your search is over. You found what you were *meant* to find. Now you must take it to Lord Asriel. Tell him that this is the weapon he needs above all others, 'Æsahættr'. Set off at once. Ignore everything else, no matter how important it may seem. Guides will show you the way. The night is full of angels.

Will moves away.

Wait. I'll never meet you again. I'm dying. Let me see what you look like.

He strikes a match. They stare at each other.

You're my son. You're Will.

An arrow strikes him, and he falls dead.

WILL Father?

Ruta Skadi appears, bow and arrow in hand.

RUTA SKADI Jopari!

WILL What have you done? I looked for him all my life, and now you've killed him. Why?

RUTA SKADI I loved him. And he rejected me, for the sake of your mother and you! I am a witch! I don't forgive! I can't forgive! Yambe-Akka, take me!

She stabs herself and dies. Will goes to his father.

WILL Father … Dad, Daddy … Father. You loved us. I'm sorry I doubted you. I'll do what you want, I swear it. I'll be the man that you want me to be. I'll fight. I'll be a warrior. I'll take this knife to Lord Asriel, wherever he is.

In the far distance, Lyra can be heard calling.

LYRA Will! Help me! She's taking me away!

WILL Lyra?

He runs back to ***the witches' encampment****. The witches are standing dead and frozen.*

Lyra! Lyra!

He finds the place where he and Lyra were sleeping.

Oh God. Oh God. She's gone.

Serafina and Kaisa are there.

SERAFINA It was the woman with the monkey daemon. She killed my witches.

KAISA All of them, all of them.

WILL Where's Lyra?

SERAFINA Her mother has taken her, Will. I arrived too late. Where were you?

WILL I found my father. And now he's dead. But he gave me a task. I've got to take this knife to Lord Asriel.

SERAFINA So the choice is yours. Either save the world, or save your friend. I know which I would do …

Kaisa stops her continuing.

But I can't help you to decide. Ruta Skadi was right. I meddled in human lives, and brought destruction on my sisters. If all goes well for you and Lyra, we'll meet on the battlefield. Farewell.

She goes. Will picks up Lyra's rucksack. He takes out the alethiometer and looks at it.

WILL Which should I choose?

Two angels – Balthamos and Baruch – appear.

Who are you?

BALTHAMOS We are angels. We have been following your father. We hoped he would lead us to you …

BARUCH … and he did.

WILL Why didn't you save him?

BARUCH We protected him all the time until he found you.

BALTHAMOS Then his task was over. Now we must lead you to Lord Asriel.

Will hesitates.

What are you waiting for?

WILL I'll do that later.

He holds out the alethiometer.

I want you to help me find the girl that this belongs to.

BARUCH Have you forgotten your father's orders?

BALTHAMOS You must ignore everything else, never mind how important it might seem.

WILL Are you stronger than me, or weaker?

BALTHAMOS Weaker. You've got flesh. We're only made of spirit.

WILL Right, then I'm telling you. Help me to find her.

BALTHAMOS Ask us politely and we may.

WILL Do you know where her mother's taken her?

BARUCH We know where she came from.

BALTHAMOS From a tent nearby with a dead man eaten by Spectres.

WILL What does he look like?

BARUCH Pasty. Silvery hair. Sixty.

WILL She's killed Lord Boreal. That's something good. One of you follow her, fast as you can. Come back and tell me where they've gone. The other one stay.

BARUCH You are making a great mistake …

BALTHAMOS … but we have no choice.

Scene 12

A cave. *Red silk prayer-scarves, a waterfall, a rainbow. Lyra is asleep. Roger's ghost appears.*

ROGER Lyra? Can you hear me?

Lyra stirs in her sleep, then half wakes up.

LYRA Rodge, where are you?

ROGER Help me, Lyra. I'm in a terrible place. It's grey, all grey. No hope, no nothing. Come to me, Lyra. Won't you rescue me?

LYRA Rodge!

Mrs Coulter comes in, carrying a bowl containing a sleeping draught. She hurries to Lyra and feeds her with a spoon.

MRS COULTER Don't be upset, my darling, it's only a dream. I've brought your medicine. It will keep you calm, it'll keep you sleeping.

Roger disappears as Lyra sleeps more deeply.

How lovely you look. Are you happy like this? I am.

Scene 13

Cittàgazze. ***Mrs Coulter's camp.*** *Will is putting things in a bag. Lord Boreal is standing dead, as when last seen. Balthamos is there.*

WILL Do you think I need anything else?

BALTHAMOS You need some inner resource to help you recognise my age-old wisdom and respect it.

WILL What's the matter? You hungry or something?

BALTHAMOS Angels don't get hungry.

WILL So you don't want any of this?

BALTHAMOS What is it?

WILL Kendal Mint Cake.

BALTHAMOS I might try a little out of interest.

Will gives him some, and Balthamos nibbles it fastidiously.

WILL Have you and your friend got names?

BALTHAMOS I am Balthamos, and my friend is Baruch.

WILL Who sent you?

BALTHAMOS We sent ourselves. We heard the rumour of Lord Asriel's war, and it inspired us to join him. But we wanted to take him something more, because we're not high-ranking in the heavenly scheme of things. We wanted to bring the knife. To see the Authority killed, and his Clouded Mountain laid to waste, is an ambition that Baruch and I have nursed for many centuries.

WILL Have you always been angels?

BALTHAMOS I was created in my present form. Baruch used to be a man.

WILL When?

BALTHAMOS Only four thousand years ago. I date from the antediluvian era, but the difference in our age is not important.

WILL So do people become angels when they die?

BALTHAMOS Mostly not. May I ask the point of this metaphysical speculation?

WILL My father's just died, that's the point. What mostly happens when people die?

BALTHAMOS They go to the world of the dead.

WILL What's it like?

BALTHAMOS It's a prison camp. That's all we know. That's all that anyone knows. The Church tells people that, if they're good, they'll go to heaven. But that's a lie.

WILL He's in a prison camp?

BALTHAMOS Of course, like the countless millions who died before him. Now that you've loaded up the dead man's property, can we move on? Baruch will be here in a matter of seconds.

WILL How do you know? Do you read his mind?

BALTHAMOS I'm *in* his mind, and he is in mine.

Baruch appears.

BARUCH Balthamos!

BALTHAMOS My heart, my own!

They embrace and hold hands.

Well?

BARUCH Lyra is in the world she came from, in a cave beneath a range of snowy mountains. I've drawn it for Will.

He produces a map. Will looks at it.

There's a waterfall where the ice and mist form rainbows. Red silk banners fly in the wind. The woman with the monkey daemon is keeping her asleep.

WILL What with?

BARUCH A potion. Lyra has not been harmed. She's dreaming.

WILL Good, so I won't need you two.

BALTHAMOS You'll need us to find Lord Asriel.

WILL No, I won't, because Lyra can read the alethiometer. All right?

BALTHAMOS No, not all right. How do we know you'll go to Lord Asriel? You've already delayed it once.

WILL Do you think I'm just gonna ignore my father, after what happened? You're not human.

BARUCH Obviously.

BALTHAMOS The notion of having a father at all is quite incomprehensible to the average angel.

BARUCH Let's compromise. I'll fly on, and tell Lord Asriel that you're on your way …

BALTHAMOS … and I shall remain with Will.

WILL I don't need *either* of you.

BALTHAMOS You do. In Lyra's world, you'll need a daemon or you'll look very much out of place. I can be one.

WILL You mean, change into a bird or something?

BALTHAMOS That is exactly what I mean. It will be unspeakably humiliating, and I'll do it only when it's absolutely essential. Wait over there.

Will picks up his bags and goes. Balthamos addresses Baruch.

BALTHAMOS It was painful to be parted from you.

BARUCH It was painful for me to be in a world of mortals. I remembered so clearly what it was like to be one myself. I longed for a body like they possess, so warm and sensuous. I envied them.

BALTHAMOS Fly with care. Lord Asriel's fortress is surrounded by enemy angels. My heart goes with you.

They embrace. Baruch flies off.

Scene 14

The Botanic Gardens. *Lyra and Will are there, as before.*

LYRA I was frightened that I'd never wake up, that I'd be stuck in the place that I was dreaming about. There was mist all round me … grey mist and a grey sky, and an enormous grey plain, trodden flat by the people there. There were millions of them, young, old, pale, dark … all crammed together, all sad and sorrowful.

WILL 'A prison camp.' The moment the angel said those words, everything changed.

LYRA Then I saw Roger. He was the only one there with hope in his eyes. He called my name and he ran to me and I tried to throw my arms around him, but they went right through the air.

WILL I could feel the words I wanted to say to my father bursting inside me. I had to see him. Had to talk to him. It was my task …

LYRA I said, 'I'll find you, Rodge. I swore it before, and I swear it again.'

WILL … It was my mantle.

Lord Roke is heard:

LORD ROKE *Lord Roke attempting contact with our Gallivespian agents in Geneva … testing, testing … come in, Chevalier, are you hearing me …?*

Scene 15

***The Consistorial Court of Discipline.** A corridor. Brother Jasper approaches the President at a run, practically tripping over his soutane. He carries the alethiometer and a handful of notes.*

Two Gallivespians, the Chevalier Tialys and Lady Salmakia, are seen eavesdropping.

BR JASPER Father President! Forgive my haste. It's the alethiometer. It's pouring out information!

PRESIDENT What has it told you?

BR JASPER Lyra Belacqua is being kept a captive … by her mother in … yes, in a cave in the mountains. They've never yet been explored, so the alethiometer wasn't able to give me a map reference … but there's a rainbow above the cave and a row of red silk flags, heathen flags, they're a method of prayer.

PRESIDENT Which world is Lyra in?

BR JASPER She's in our world. And so is the boy.

PRESIDENT The *boy*?

BR JASPER That's what I came running to tell you. There's a boy, the bearer of the knife we spoke of. He's Lyra's friend. He's *part of her story*. It seems the prophecy's moving even faster than we feared.

PRESIDENT We must pray that we have enough time to counteract it. Have you assembled the band of brothers, as I told you?

BR JASPER I have.

PRESIDENT Are they skilled in combat, staunch in belief and willing to lose their lives for the holy purpose?

BR JASPER They are, Father President. So am I.

PRESIDENT Then it falls to you, Brother Jasper, to save us from the doom that threatens us all. Find out the precise location of the cave. Once you have done so, you and your holy brethren will approach it by zeppelin. What you must do there will be hard for you. Your whole nature will rise up in revolt. Subdue it. By killing the child before she can be tempted, you will save her soul. Kneel.

Brother Jasper does. The President takes a medallion from around his neck and places it round Brother Jasper's.

This sacred medallion of Saint Martin Luther absolves the wearer from every crime, past and present. Wear it for Lyra. Come.

Scene 16

As he and Brother Jasper leave, the Chevalier Tialys and Lady Salmakia relay a message on their lodestone resonator. We cross-fade to Lord Asriel's fortress: **the war room.** ***Aides and officers are studying maps, plotting battle positions, etc. Lord Asriel and Lord Roke see Lord Tialys's message as it appears.***

TIALYS *... Your loyal spies present their compliments from Geneva ... ... the*

Church's alethiometer is now dangerously effective thanks to skilful reader …

LORD ASRIEL And?

TIALYS *… a boy has taken the knife from Cittàgazze, into the daemon-world …*

LORD ASRIEL To where exactly?

TIALYS *… news of your daughter, however, is more abundant …*

LORD ASRIEL Lord Roke, are these spies of yours any good?

LORD ROKE They are Gallivespians of ancient lineage, my lord. I hope you do not equate small size with small ability.

SALMAKIA *… Lyra is in a cave in the Northern mountains … her mother is keeping her in a trance …*

LORD ASRIEL Her mother? Stuck in a cave? I don't believe it. This is a woman who has her hair done twice a week at six in the morning.

TIALYS *… the Church will send a band of assassins to the cave by zeppelin. Their orders will be to eliminate Lyra without delay. Transmission over.*

LORD ASRIEL Eliminate Lyra? Why? She's not important. She's just a foul-mouthed brat with grubby fingernails. Why are they trying to kill her?

STELMARIA You'd have killed her yourself, at Svalbard.

LORD ASRIEL No, I would not! I thought I'd *have* to kill her, for the sake of my experiment. When the boy walked in, I was vastly relieved and

I let her go. But I can't help wondering now if that was a fatal error. Should I have kept her with me? Should I have brought her here?

An officer bursts in.

OFFICER My lord! An angel has arrived! An angel to join your army.

All in the room are jubilant. Baruch appears, badly wounded. The soldiers present are awe-struck: this is the first angel any of them have seen.

BARUCH Greetings, Lord Asriel.

LORD ASRIEL You're wounded!

BARUCH I was attacked by enemy angels on my way here. I will not live to fight for you. Others will come to you, they will flock in their millions. I'm just a messenger.

He stops to collect his strength. Lord Asriel turns away.

LORD ASRIEL Well?

BARUCH The knife … 'Æsahættr' …

Lord Asriel turns to look at him. Tense.

LORD ASRIEL Do you know where it is?

BARUCH Jopari has sent it to you. His warrior son will bring it …

LORD ASRIEL When will he come?

BARUCH I don't know. He disobeyed his father's orders … he's gone …

LORD ASRIEL Where?

BARUCH … he's gone to the cave where your daughter is held a prisoner. Bring me a map, I can show you …

Somebody does.

LORD ROKE It's too late, my lord. His light is fading.

Baruch points to a place on the map.

LORD ASRIEL No, he's pointing.

BARUCH Oh, Balthamos!

He dies.

LORD ASRIEL The paper is cold where his finger touched it. The cave is here. Lord Roke, order our spies in Geneva to conceal themselves in one of the Church's aircraft. They will brief you hourly on the enemy's plan of attack. And order six gyropters ready to take to the air at once.

LORD ROKE Who will command them?

LORD ASRIEL I shall. I'll fly to the cave. I'll capture the knife and save my daughter.

STELMARIA So do you care about her?

LORD ASRIEL Yes I do! It's like a chess game, when you suddenly realise that your opponent is concentrating all his energies on capturing some insignificant little piece to which you had never attached the remotest value. You don't know why he wants it. But if it matters to him, then it matters to you. You have to defend it.

Scene 17

Lyra's world. ***Snowy foothills****. Will and Balthamos are travelling.*

BALTHAMOS Baruch is dead! Baruch is dead!

He flies into the air.

WILL Balthamos! Don't leave me! I need you!

But Balthamos has disappeared. Will gets out a map and studies it. Bears appear and approach him with hungry eyes. Will turns and sees them.

What do you want?

The bears confer among themselves.

1ST BEAR What is it?

2ND BEAR It's got no daemon.

3RD BEAR Is it spirit or flesh?

The 1st Bear touches Will.

1ST BEAR It's flesh!

BEARS It's meat! It's food! Food! Food!

WILL Get back! I've got a knife!

BEARS A knife!

They laugh derisively. Iorek appears.

IOREK What's this?

1ST BEAR It's a warm-blooded creature, Your Majesty. We don't know what it is, but we've not eaten for days. We're starving!

The bears bellow with hunger.

ALL BEARS Kill him!/We're hungry!/We want to eat!

WILL You can't eat me! I'm a human being!

The bears roar angrily.

IOREK That's the worst thing you could have said!

BEARS We hate humans!

IOREK It was a human woman who corrupted Svalbard! It was a human man who blew a hole in the sky and let the sun in! So why should you be spared, you shivering sprat, you pale-faced porpoise, you two-legged shrimp?

A chorus of agreement from the bears.

WILL I'll show you. I challenge you to fight me in single combat.

The bears roar with laughter.

If I lose, you can kill me and eat me, whatever you like. But if I win … you've got to take me up to the mountains. You've got to stay with me, and fight for me whenever I tell you.

IOREK I will not fight you! It would be shameful! You are as weak as an oyster out of its shell.

WILL You're right! I am! It's not a fair contest at all. You've got all that armour, and I've got none. You could take off my head with one sweep of your paw. Make it fairer. Give me one piece of your armour, any bit you like. Then we'll be evenly matched, and there won't be any shame in fighting me.

IOREK Take this.

With a snarl, he removes his helmet and throws it down at Will's feet. Will picks it up and looks at it carefully.

WILL So this is your armour? It doesn't look very strong to me. Let me see.

He draws the knife and slices up the helmet. The bears mutter in fear.

Well, that was your armour. And this is my knife. And since your helmet wasn't any use to me, I'll have to fight you without it. Are you ready, bear? I think we're well matched. I could take off your head with one sweep of my knife, after all.

IOREK It is too strong a weapon. I can't fight it. Boy, you win.

The bears growl in recognition.

Now show it to me.

WILL I will only show this knife to a bear I've heard about, who I know I can trust. He's the king of the bears, and a good friend of the girl I'm going to the mountains to look for. Her name is Lyra Silvertongue. The bear is called Iorek Byrnison.

IOREK I am Iorek Byrnison.

WILL I know you are.

He holds out the knife.

Here, hold it carefully.

He hands Iorek the knife. Iorek looks at it.

IOREK This is the edge you cut my armour with. It's sharp enough.

He turns it over.

But *this* edge is the most fearful thing I've ever seen. I can't tell what it is, or how it was made. How did you come by it?

WILL I won it in a fight. I'm taking it to use in a war on Lord Asriel's side. But first, I've got to rescue Lyra.

He unfolds the map.

She's being held a prisoner in a cave, and it's somewhere up that river and in these mountains.

IOREK That's where we bears are travelling. We've lost our hunting grounds. The ocean is warm, the seals have died, the ice is melting. But I have heard that in those mountains, there are wild creatures a-plenty and snows that last forever. Come with us.

The bears roar in approval. Balthamos appears.

BALTHAMOS Forgive me, Will. I was disabled by my grief. But one must do what is right, even after you've lost the one you love.

IOREK Who is this?

WILL It's Balthamos. He's an angel. This is Iorek Byrnison, the king of the Svalbard bears.

IOREK We've heard of angels. We see them as points of light in the Northern skies. But never before have I met one face to face.

BALTHAMOS Nor I a bear.

IOREK Let's go!

They go.

Scene 18

*Geneva: **The Consistorial Court of Discipline.** Brother Jasper addresses an assembly.*

BR JASPER Fellow-warriors of the Brotherhood of the Holy Purpose! I, your leader, will now confide in you our plan of action.

A map of Lyra's world appears.

First, the greater picture. This is our world. There at Svalbard is the huge connecting route that Lord Asriel blasted through into Cittàgazze … with the environmental consequences that we've seen … melting ice caps, rising sea levels, the opening up of random windows too many to be displayed and a vast increase in the draining away of Dust.

A map of Cittàgazze appears.

I'm showing the worlds side by side because it's clearer like this, although in life, of course, they occupy the identical space. Lyra followed Lord Asriel through here into Cittàgazze, while he moved on to the strange, anonymous, astral world in which he's built his fortress.

A map of our world appears. Other maps follow as needed.

There's a window *here* between Cittàgazze and a curious world that boasts a parallel Oxford, very like ours. Lord Boreal used to take this route before the Spectres arrived in such vast numbers, and so did Will and Lyra in their journeyings round the knife. *This* is a derelict Arctic gap, discovered twelve years ago by the shaman Jopari, who has thankfully now been killed. *This* is the window through which Mrs Coulter carried Lyra back to our world, and into the cave of rainbows. *That* is the cave!

He points it out.

Lord Asriel is leading a force of six gyropters through his Svalbard window, and they will shortly approach the cave from *here*. The boy with the knife was taken upriver by the king of the armoured bears, and they will arrive from *here*. We shall advance by zeppelin from *this* direction and arrive at the cave at the same time as our enemies. The battle will follow. The advantage is to us, because Lord Asriel will be trying to carry his daughter home alive, whereas our aim can be achieved with two strokes of the sword: one for the girl, and one for the boy. The second great prize, the knife, will then be ours. In brief, dear brothers in faith, dear holy pilgrims, you who will survive the battle with lifelong honour, you who will fall and rise to a blissful eternity, we depart on a sacred mission. We shall save Lyra Belacqua from the damnation of the witches' prophecy. We shall save the world!

Applause.

Scene 19

Near the cave. Will, Iorek and Balthamos arrive, accompanied by other bears.

IOREK Listen!

They do.

Zeppelins are approaching from the South.

WILL Ssh.

He listens.

What's that?

IOREK Gyropters from the North. We must rescue Lyra now, before they attack.

BALTHAMOS The cave is there.

WILL Right, this is what we'll do. I'll go to the cave. I'll wait till it's empty. Then I'll wake up Lyra …

BALTHAMOS A great mistake!

WILL I've done it before, all right? I'll cut a window, then I'll bring her back through a different world …

BALTHAMOS Her mother might find you.

WILL What if she does? She can't do anything.

BALTHAMOS She can do much.

IOREK She will enchant you, like she enchanted Iofur Raknison.

WILL Me? Get enchanted by her? Yes, that's *really* likely, after she kidnapped Lyra, and slagged me off to that poncey pal of hers … and then she *killed* him! I'm not going to hang about, you can be sure of that. Just keep an eye out for the monkey.

He walks to ***the cave*** *and goes in. Lyra is there, asleep.*

Lyra? Lyra! Sit up.

She remains asleep. He eases her up.

That's right. Come on. I'm cutting us out.

With one arm around Lyra, he reaches out with the knife to cut a window. Mrs Coulter appears at the mouth of the cave, with her bowl of medicine.

MRS COULTER Will! Thank God you're here.

WILL How did you know who I am?

MRS COULTER Who else would be so brave as to come at a time like this? We've not a moment to lose. Quick, cut a window into another world, and we'll all go through.

WILL All?

MRS COULTER Yes, all. Lyra, you and me.

WILL Stay where you are! I'm rescuing her, not you.

MRS COULTER Why not?

WILL Because she wouldn't want you anywhere near her. She hates you. Didn't you know that? Keep away!

He holds out the knife, ready to cut a window.

MRS COULTER Is that the knife?

WILL Yeah, ten out of ten.

MRS COULTER Let me look at it.

WILL No! Be quiet!

MRS COULTER Why?

WILL Because the knife could break if …

MRS COULTER What?

WILL Nothing.

MRS COULTER Do you mean, if you were distracted?

WILL Forget I said it. Lyra. Lyra, stand up. We're going.

MRS COULTER Take me too.

WILL No! You've got a nerve even to ask, when it was you that kidnapped Lyra and made her a prisoner.

MRS COULTER I had to. She's in danger from the Church.

WILL She knows that! She's escaped them over and over again. She didn't need any help from you. She never asked *you* to turn her into a pet, a zombie! Look, I'm not arguing, right? 'Cause that's exactly what you want. Keep away.

He prepares once again to cut a window, but has difficulty concentrating.

MRS COULTER You're right, she hates me. Even after all the sacrifices I've made for her. I've had to cut myself off from the Church, the Church that has comforted and supported me all my life. But I must protect my daughter. And if that means keeping her fast asleep, so be it. Wouldn't *your* mother do the same for you? Wouldn't she, Will?

Will turns to her.

WILL You don't know anything about my mother.

MRS COULTER I'm sure she looks after you.

Will is angry and upset.

WILL I look after her, as it happens. Shut up about her.

Aircraft are directly overhead.

MRS COULTER They're here. Cut the window. Cut it and let us all through. Now!

Sounds of approaching battle.

WILL Stand back! I'm taking Lyra!

Mrs Coulter produces a revolver and aims it at Will.

MRS COULTER Stay where you are! I'm holding you captive!

The Chevalier Tialys and Lady Salmakia appear beside her.

WILL What, as hostages?

MRS COULTER Yes, hostages! They all want the knife and they all want Lyra! You're my only chance!

The Gallivespians sting her ankle. She screams and falls to the ground.

I've been stung! It's agony!

She sees the Gallivespians.

What are those *things*!

Lyra starts to wake.

LYRA What's happening? Where are we?

WILL You've been asleep. Come on. Get up.

He poises the knife.

LYRA Oh, Will, I had an amazing dream.

WILL Don't talk. We're getting out. Hold on to me tight.

He tries to find a snag in the air. The cave is invaded by Brothers of the Holy Purpose. They advance on Lyra and Will. Lord Asriel appears, with a troupe of his soldiers.

MRS COULTER Asriel!

LORD ASRIEL Lyra!

LYRA No! Go away!

Lord Asriel and his soldiers attack the Brothers. Meanwhile:

LYRA It's him! It's my dad! Cut a window, quick!

Will stands poised to do so, trying to concentrate.

MRS COULTER Lyra, don't go!

WILL Don't talk to her.

MRS COULTER My precious, my dear one. Help me!

WILL Quiet!

MRS COULTER Lyra, don't leave me here to die.

WILL Tell her to shut up. If I don't concentrate, the knife's gonna break.

Lord Asriel breaks from the fighting and addresses Will:

LORD ASRIEL Will! Give me the knife!

LYRA Don't listen to him! Cut a window!

LORD ASRIEL Give it to me!

LYRA Go away! Cut a window! Will!

WILL I'm trying.

He tries with all his might to concentrate.

LORD ASRIEL Will! Do as your father told you! Think of your father! *Think of your father!*

WILL Dad?

The knife shatters. More Holy Brothers invade the cave. Lord Asriel fights them off while protecting Lyra. Balthamos is seen fleeing in a panic. Under cover of the fighting, Will picks up the pieces of the knife and pulls Lyra away and out of the cave. Lord Asriel looks round and sees that she has gone.

LORD ASRIEL Lyra! Lyra!

Act Two

Scene 1

***Lord Asriel's fortress.** Lord Asriel, alone.*

LORD ASRIEL I dreamt last night of the angel who challenged the Authority all those aeons ago. The angel who failed because the knife that could deliver the death-blow hadn't yet been invented. I was falling with him down an endless abyss, into a blackness so intense that it seemed to invade my brain. But I could feel the rush of his wings beside me, and I asked him … did he know, had he suspected … that from this night on, he would be held responsible for everything bad that ever happened … every temptation, every atrocity, every crime? He laughed. He said he wasn't surprised at all. He knew the system. The recording angels always put the blame on the losing side. And then I woke, and remembered that the knife was broken.

*Lord Asriel's fortress. **The war room**. Aides and officers pause in their work to watch the latest dispatch from the Gallivespians. Lord Asriel listens, his hand on Stelmaria. Lord Roke operates the receiving equipment.*

TIALYS … *The Chevalier Tialys and Lady Salmakia report from the site of the recent battle.*

LORD ASRIEL Have they found my daughter?

TIALYS *Our tour of the surroundings reveals heavy losses by the enemy …*

SALMAKIA *... young men in clerical garb who had adopted near-suicidal tactics.*

LORD ASRIEL But why?

SALMAKIA *On the body of one, we found these battle orders ...*

She holds up a piece of paper.

... of which the final sentence is of interest:

She reads it out:

'We shall save Lyra Belacqua from the damnation of the witches' prophecy. We shall save the world!'

LORD ASRIEL A prophecy? I was right. She *is* important. But where is she now?

LORD ROKE I think we're coming to that, my lord.

TIALYS *Lyra and the boy emerged from their hiding place after the close of fighting. We are observing them, and will shortly bring them to your Lordship's fortress by gyropter.*

The Gallivespians' image fades.

LORD ASRIEL She'll soon be here.

STELMARIA Don't be too sure.

LORD ROKE I'd like to echo your daemon's doubts, my lord. It's the absence of the knife that worries me most. Even the broken pieces would be better than nothing. I wonder why your lordship didn't collect them?

LORD ASRIEL What, scrabble in the dirt to pick them up? I wouldn't demean the knife like that. I wouldn't demean myself, or the boy either.

He'll bring me the useless remains when the time is right, and on his own terms. That's how it must be.

LORD ROKE A sentiment after my own heart, my lord! We Gallivespians have few victories to our name but, by golly, we lose with honour!

Scene 2

Lyra's world. ***Near the cave.*** *Lyra and Will are there.*

LYRA You mean, your father was Jopari?

WILL Yeah, that's right! And he gave me the knife and he told me to take it to Lord Asriel. But I put that off for a bit so I could rescue you, and I was brought here by some apology for an angel who went screaming off the minute the fighting started. Then your father arrived, and that's when the *real* disaster happened.

LYRA Let's see it.

He lays out the shattered pieces of the knife. She looks at them.

One, two, three, four …

WILL Seven pieces. It was your dad. He made me think about my own father … and my thoughts got split, and the knife came up against something hard. And I forced it, and it flew into pieces.

LYRA Iorek can fix it.

WILL Can he? Can he really?

LYRA Yeah, I bet he can! He can do more with metal than any bear alive, he told me. Come on, let's find him.

The Chevalier Tialys and Lady Salmakia appear.

WILL Hang on a minute. Look!

LYRA Wow.

WILL Are they normal size and far away?

LYRA No, they're under our noses and they're tiny.

TIALYS Good morning, Lyra. Good morning, Master Will.

WILL Who are you?

LYRA Whose side are you on?

TIALYS I am the Chevalier Tialys, and this is my spouse, the Lady Salmakia. We are Gallivespians, and Lord Asriel's trusted spies.

SALMAKIA We have been searching for you, Miss Lyra, at your father's command. *(to Tialys)* Will you continue, my lord?

TIALYS I yield to you, my lady.

SALMAKIA Too kind. Our orders are to take you to your father's fortress without delay. A gyropter will shortly arrive to collect us.

LYRA What if I don't wanna go?

TIALYS Our powers of persuasion are not inconsiderable. Have you forgotten the Gallivespians' notorious sting?

WILL What about me? I've got an important message for Lord Asriel.

TIALYS Your message is of no value, now that the knife is broken.

SALMAKIA Which it certainly seems to be.

The Gallivespians look at the pieces of the knife, which are still spread out.

WILL Yeah, I agree it looks pretty terrible. But there's an armoured bear, called Iorek Byrnison …

Lyra interrupts hastily.

LYRA It's just broken bits of metal, isn't it? And the thing about the bear is, we just wanna say goodbye to him. Will you fetch him for us please?

TIALYS Stay here, and we shall bring him to you.

SALMAKIA But once we have done so, you must travel directly to Lord Asriel.

LYRA Oh, I'll do that all right.

The Gallivespians go.

You're a hopeless, useless liar, Will. It's lucky I'm here. It's really important that those gallipot-things don't know it's gonna be fixed.

WILL Why not?

LYRA 'Cause I don't wanna go to my father's, right? 'Cause he killed Roger. And there's something else that I gotta do, and that's about Roger too. I gotta rescue him.

WILL Roger's dead!

LYRA I know, but I seen him, Will. All that time I was asleep, I kept on having a dream. I was in this huge, grey, flat nothing of a place, and Roger was there. He was … beckoning to me, calling me, only I couldn't hear him. And he's only *there* because of me … and if I could find him, I could help him escape. Only I don't know where he is.

WILL He's in the land of the dead.

LYRA How do you know?

WILL The angel told me. He said my father's gone there too.

LYRA Then you gotta come with me, Will! We'll find them *both*! An' you can help your dad get out of that horrible place. You'll do it, won't you?

WILL Yeah … I will … 'cause there's something I want to say to him, and I only thought of it when it was too late.

PANTALAIMON How will you get there?

WILL The knife'll cut us into it.

LYRA Course it will!

PANTALAIMON But …

WILL Look, here's Iorek.

Iorek is there.

IOREK Lyra Silvertongue! You sent for me.

LYRA Yeah, Will's got something very special to ask you.

WILL Ssh, ssh, ssh, hang on. Can you see those little whatsits anywhere?

They look round.

LYRA No, they've gone.

WILL You sure about that?

LYRA Quite sure.

IOREK What is your question?

Will shows him the broken pieces of the knife.

WILL Can you mend this knife?

LYRA I know you can!

Tialys and Salmakia appear from somewhere unexpected.

SALMAKIA This bear can mend it?

TIALYS You've deceived us!

SALMAKIA It was dishonourable to lie.

WILL Well, you never asked permission to interrupt. This bear happens to be a king, and you're just a couple of spies.

LYRA And if you knew that we was lying, you'd have probably killed us.

WILL And we'd never have found the only creature in the world who can actually fix it!

IOREK *(severely to the Gallivespians)* Well?

TIALYS Forgive us, Your Majesty. The habit of concealment is hard to break. In our world, we live amongst larger humans who are constantly attempting to exterminate us. Our intentions towards yourself are wholly respectful.

SALMAKIA We only intend to take these children to Lord Asriel.

TIALYS And the knife as well.

SALMAKIA Once it is mended.

IOREK Let me see it.

Will shows him the pieces. He looks at them.

I didn't trust this knife when I saw it before. I still don't like it. It would be better if it had never been made.

LYRA Oh, Iorek, if you only knew what we wanted to do with it …

IOREK Your intentions may be good. But the knife has its own intentions. In doing what *you* want, you may also do what the knife wants, without your knowing it. Look at this edge. Can you see where it ends?

LYRA/WILL No.

IOREK Then how can you know where it will take you?

LYRA I can ask the alethiometer.

IOREK Ask it now. Then, if you still want me to mend it for you, I will do so.

TIALYS May I respectfully say, Your Majesty, that the knife must be repaired whatever the child decides.

SALMAKIA But we must not pre-empt the King.

TIALYS How true, my dear. Let us withdraw to send Lord Asriel our dispatch.

They go.

LYRA Can they hear us?

WILL No.

She reads the alethiometer. Iorek watches.

IOREK What does it say?

LYRA It's … confused. It says the knife could be harmful, but it can also do good. But it's a tiny difference, like the littlest thought could tip it one way or the other.

WILL What does it say about … the plan we made?

LYRA It says it's dangerous.

WILL What if we don't go?

LYRA Just … blankness. Emptiness. Nothing.

WILL How do we get there?

LYRA It says, 'Follow the knife'.

IOREK And is that what you want?

LYRA It is.

IOREK Then you must help me. Empty your mind of everything but the knife. Remember it as it was. I'll build a fire.

Scene 3

Lord Asriel's fortress. *Lord Asriel, with Stelmaria at his side, receives a message from the Chevalier Tialys. Lord Roke is there.*

TIALYS *… The news is bad and good …*

SALMAKIA *… the knife is about to be repaired by an armoured bear, King Iorek Byrnison.*

LORD ASRIEL Repaired?

TIALYS *Lyra and the boy have promised to bring it to you once it is mended …*

The room erupts in triumph, as:

LORD ASRIEL Yes! I've got it!

LORD ROKE There's more, my lord.

SALMAKIA *But they are lying to us …*

LORD ASRIEL What?

SALMAKIA … *they plan instead to travel to some unspecified location and to take it with them. Transmission over.*

LORD ASRIEL The boy's betrayed me. Lord Roke, tell your spies to sting him to death, and bring me the knife themselves.

LORD ROKE No, that won't help, my lord. The knife is only effective in the hand of the Bearer.

LORD ASRIEL Then they must bring him here by force.

LORD ROKE No, that's not possible. Once the knife is in working order, he can't be forced to do anything. We've reached a deadlock.

Lord Asriel flies into a rage.

LORD ASRIEL Damn those children! Damn the boy!

An officer appears at the door.

OFFICER My lord, the prisoner insists on seeing you.

LORD ASRIEL Not now! Send her away!

Mrs Coulter appears, her hands tied.

MRS COULTER Bound! Gagged! Dragged through your corridors like a criminal!

LORD ASRIEL Oh, bring her in. Somebody free her. Everyone else, clear the room.

Officers bring her in. Mrs Coulter protests to the officer untying her.

MRS COULTER Gently! Gently!

LORD ASRIEL Calm down!

MRS COULTER Calm down? Don't you dare patronise me.

The officer untying her is the last person there. To him:

Out!

To Asriel:

Where's our daughter? What have you done with her?

LORD ASRIEL I haven't done anything. She's back in the cave, where you saw her last.

MRS COULTER You left her behind? While the battle was raging?

LORD ASRIEL I would have rescued her if she'd had the wit to allow me to. But she ran away. Both she and the boy. They hid.

MRS COULTER Didn't you look for her?

LORD ASRIEL Of course I looked! Use your intelligence, Marisa. Why do you think I went to the cave in the first place?

MRS COULTER Not for her. You've never minded whether she lived or died.

LORD ASRIEL But now I do.

MRS COULTER Well then, you'd better go back and get her.

LORD ASRIEL I can't.

MRS COULTER Why not?

LORD ASRIEL Because like any other pair of selfish, self-indulgent children, they've placed their own concerns above the good of everyone else.

MRS COULTER Just what does that mean exactly?

LORD ASRIEL They plan to escape.

MRS COULTER Escape from you, you mean.

LORD ASRIEL And you.

MRS COULTER So … where are they going?

LORD ASRIEL I've no idea.

MRS COULTER Has it crossed your mind that as long as Lyra is wandering free she'll be in terrible danger?

LORD ASRIEL I know that.

MRS COULTER *Now* you know it. Now you *admit* it. I tried to tell you that at Svalbard and you said I was talking nonsense.

LORD ASRIEL That was nothing! There was a zeppelin overhead! A single zeppelin! It's different now. The Church is obsessed with her. They sent a party of suicide killers to wipe her out. What's the prophecy?

MRS COULTER The prophecy?

LORD ASRIEL Yes, the witches' prophecy. What is it?

MRS COULTER There's a name. A secret name. That name is the key to whether or not she's the Church's greatest enemy, and it's perfectly obvious that they've found it out and decided that she is.

LORD ASRIEL Do you know this name?

MRS COULTER I wish I did. I wish I thought that it mattered to you. You've never shown the remotest interest in her.

LORD ASRIEL Why do you keep saying that? All I can think about, all I care about, night and day, is to find and protect that child who is so dear to us both.

MRS COULTER I don't know why I believe you. You always lied in the past. I always knew it. But something's dulled in me. I've changed. Lyra has changed me. All those nights in the cave, feeding her, guarding her, listening in fear to every rustle of the wind … Well, that's all over.

She flexes her wrists.

So. We need that name, in order to fight the Church on equal terms. And we need to know where Lyra is, so you can bring her to safety. I think I'm getting somewhere. Who found the cave? Who knew that Will was there and the knife was there?

LORD ASRIEL The Church's new alethiometer reader.

MRS COULTER Exactly. I've seen him. He's called Brother Jasper, and he's young and chillingly conscientious and there's nothing he can't find out. Can't your spies in Geneva sneak into his study and peek over his shoulder?

LORD ASRIEL I haven't got any spies in Geneva. They're still at the cave. You saw them.

MRS COULTER I *experienced* them.

She rubs her ankle.

Then you must send another spy. Someone who knows how their disgusting minds work … and whom they trust, up to a point. It will have to be me.

LORD ASRIEL You? No, Marisa, it's impossible.

MRS COULTER Oh, you're worried about my safety, are you?

LORD ASRIEL I'm worried about your loyalty to me. You're the Church's faithful servant.

MRS COULTER Not any more. I hate them. I hate them so intensely that it will be difficult for me to lie to them. But I'll manage it somehow. And I'll twist little Brother Jasper into telling me all he knows. I think I'll rather enjoy that. How do I get there?

LORD ASRIEL My men will fly you there as soon as you're ready. They'll collect you the following morning at four a.m.

MRS COULTER One moment.

She looks at her monkey daemon, who is making stabbing gestures in the air.

What?

He repeats the gesture. To Lord Asriel:

Just tell me one thing. What happened to the knife?

LORD ASRIEL The knife?

MRS COULTER Yes, after it broke.

LORD ASRIEL It will be mended.

MRS COULTER *That's* what you're after, isn't it? *Isn't it?* You toad! You schemer! This is nothing to do with Lyra at all. It's the knife!

LORD ASRIEL I need that knife!

MRS COULTER What for? So you can kill the Authority? Ha ha ha. What good will that do? Have you thought about that? No, you don't care. It's all your pride, your glorification, your ambition …!

LORD ASRIEL This is unworthy of you, Marisa.

MRS COULTER Oh, come off it. How would you know what's worthy or not? You tried to exploit my motherly love for your own selfish purposes!

He laughs.

Don't laugh!

LORD ASRIEL I can't help it!

He laughs.

Your motherly love! You hated Lyra! You abandoned her!

MRS COULTER I did not! You stole her from me …!

LORD ASRIEL I had to! You were raving mad! You'd have throttled her in her cradle!

MRS COULTER … then you ignored her, you neglected her, year after year, she had no decent company, no education …

LORD ASRIEL You only loved her in that cave because she was fast asleep.

MRS COULTER What if I did? It's still love.

LORD ASRIEL No, it's not. It's fantasising. So that you won't have to *pretend* to love the tedious little creature that she really is.

MRS COULTER You know nothing about her! She's unique!

LORD ASRIEL Oh, she's unique all right. To win you round ... you of all people ... the steely eyed fanatic, the persecutor of children, the inventor of hideous machines to slice them apart ... to turn you into a fussy red hen, clucking and settling your feathers over her ... that's quite an achievement.

MRS COULTER It is.

LORD ASRIEL And you'll go to Geneva?

MRS COULTER I will. For her.

She turns to go.

Who won that? You or me?

LORD ASRIEL We both got what we wanted.

MRS COULTER So we did. But I'll be back. And then let battle commence.

She goes out. Lord Roke, who has been hiding somewhere, appears.

LORD ROKE My lord?

LORD ASRIEL Hide in the aircraft. Don't let her see you. Report to me when you get there.

Scene 4

***In the cave.** Iorek is mending the knife. Lyra, Will and Pantalaimon are helping. To Will:*

IOREK Last piece! Hold it still in your mind!

Will concentrates on his mental image of the knife.

WILL I've got it! I can see it!

IOREK Feel the atoms! Feel them joining, strengthening, straightening!

WILL I feel them!

Iorek hammers the last fragments into place.

IOREK Now it must cool. Lyra, call me when the blade turns back to silver.

He places it in the cinders. To Will:

Come.

He and Will walk out of the cave.

What will you do with the knife?

WILL I don't know.

Iorek knocks him over.

IOREK Answer me truthfully.

Will struggles to his feet.

WILL We want to go down to the land of the dead … for my father, and Roger as well. But I'm pulled in so many different ways. My mum's ill, and I want to go home and look after her. My father told me to take the knife to Lord Asriel. And I'm frightened … and maybe my fear is pushing me in the wrong direction. Maybe sometimes the frightening thing is the wrong thing, but we don't want to look like a coward, and so we do it *because* it's frightening.

IOREK I too am full of doubt. And that is a human thing. If I am becoming human, something's wrong, something's bad. It may be that I have brought the final destruction on my kingdom. But there is one thing I know for certain. If you want to succeed in the task you have set yourself, you must no longer think about your father and mother. If your mind is divided, the knife will break once more, and I will not be there to mend it.

Lyra approaches.

LYRA Iorek, the knife is ready.

IOREK Will has told me where you are going.

LYRA I've gotta rescue Roger.

IOREK Your business is not with death. It is with living creatures.

LYRA Our business is to do what we promised, en't it? I wish I'd never had that dream, and I wish we'd never found out that the knife could take us there. But it can.

IOREK Can is not the same as must.

LYRA But if you must, and you can, then you got no excuse.

IOREK I was right to call you Lyra Silvertongue. You've made me change my mind.

To Will:

Take the knife, and plunge it into the stream.

Will goes to do so. To Lyra:

When I first met him, he was too clever for me, too daring. There is no one else I would be happy to leave you with. If you escape from the land of the dead, you will meet me in the battle at the end of the world. If you cannot escape, you'll never see me again. I have no ghost. When I die, my body will lie on the earth, and then be part of it. Go well.

LYRA Go well, King Iorek Byrnison.

She embraces him and he goes. Will comes back with the knife.

WILL It's done. It'll work.

She looks at it.

LYRA It isn't beautiful any more.

WILL It looks what it is. It's wounded.

He prepares to cut a window.

You ready?

PANTALAIMON What if you can't get out?

LYRA If it can cut us in, it'll cut us out again.

PANTALAIMON What if you gotta die to be there?

WILL We aren't gonna die. Not with our bodies. 'Cause bodies don't go anywhere. They just stay in the earth and rot.

LYRA And it can't be our daemons either. They just fade and dissolve.

PANTALAIMON I don't wanna fade and dissolve!

LYRA You won't have to, Pan, 'cause there must be a different part. A part that's not our bodies, an' not our daemons. A part that can think about both those things. A third part.

WILL Our ghost.

LYRA That's right. Our ghost. We're going as ghosts.

PANTALAIMON Ghosts are sad! Ghosts are frightening! Don't go!

LYRA Oh, Pan … we won't know anything till we try it. You know I love you. I'll look after you for ever an' ever. But we can't be too frightened to do what we've got to.

WILL Let's go.

He tries a snag in the air: it feels wrong.

Not that.

Tialys and Salmakia appear.

TIALYS Where do you think you are going, young man?

LYRA Oh, no!

WILL We're gonna follow the knife to the land of the dead.

TIALYS You may not do that!

SALMAKIA You must wait for the gyropter.

WILL It doesn't matter what you think. We're going. You can come if you like, or stay where you are. It's up to you.

He stretches out his hand, holding the knife. Tries a couple of snags.

Not that. Not that.

As he looks for a place to cut, Tialys and Salmakia try to stop him.

TIALYS ***(simultaneously with Salmakia)*** This is forbidden. The entire destiny of the universe is at stake. You must follow Lord Asriel's orders. We are speaking on his behalf. You may not defy us. You must carry out your mission. You may not deviate, not in the slightest. It is rank insubordination. It is tantamount to treason. You will regret it! You'll be very, very sorry unless you stop at once! Put down that knife! Stop this immediately! Stop it at once! This instant!

SALMAKIA You may not do this. It is a direct contravention of the rules for prisoners. Put down that knife immediately. You are in our custody. You must do precisely as we command you. We have explained this very clearly. How dare you be so disobedient? How dare you? Don't you know who we are? It's an outrage. It's atrocious behaviour. You have brought disgrace on the entire Gallivespian nation. We shall punish you frightfully. I order you to do as we say! Do as we say!

Will tries another.

WILL This could be it.

The feeling is unpleasant.

You sure about this?

LYRA Go on.

He cuts a window. They stare in amazement at what they see through it.

Scene 5

A* lodestone resonator *signal from Tialys.

TIALYS *The Chevalier Tialys regrets to inform you … Lyra and the boy have escaped with the knife to the Land of the Dead after overpowering your agents and issuing violent threats …*

The signal cross-fades with another signal.

LORD ROKE *Lord Roke reporting from Geneva … Mrs Coulter arrived purporting to bring vital information damaging to your lordship. This claim was greeted with mistrust. She has been placed in a cell, where the President will shortly arrive to interrogate her.*

The Consistorial Court of Discipline. Mrs Coulter is in* a cell. *She's about to undress when she sees Lord Roke.

MRS COULTER Lord Roke! Just when would you have done me the courtesy of telling me you were here? Before I undressed or after?

LORD ROKE Before, of course. Do you really suppose I have some unseemly interest in giantesses? I've toured the grounds. They're preparing for war. The priests are taking it in relays to warn the Authority.

MRS COULTER How?

LORD ROKE Incense, bells, whatever they can lay their hands on.

MRS COULTER Has Brother Jasper found out where Lyra is?

LORD ROKE I think not yet. He's looking worried.

A knock at the door.

See for yourself.

MRS COULTER Quick, hide.

Lord Roke conceals himself.

Come in.

The President and Brother Jasper enter.

PRESIDENT Welcome, Mrs Coulter. Forgive this simple hospitality. Once you have proved that you are truly the Church's friend, and not a traitor, you'll have better lodgings.

MRS COULTER *(to Brother Jasper)* I believe we've met.

PRESIDENT Brother Jasper is here to ensure that I do not waste our time by asking you questions which can be more swiftly answered by the alethiometer.

MRS COULTER Well, he's a great improvement on Fra Pavel, in all sorts of ways. I'm so sorry. Ask me whatever you like.

PRESIDENT I'm bound to wonder how you escaped from Lord Asriel's fortress with such ease, and how you came to Geneva?

MRS COULTER As I told your guards, I stole a gyropter. I landed it in the countryside not far from here, and the rest of the way I walked.

PRESIDENT What can you tell me about the mysterious disappearance of Lord Boreal?

MRS COULTER He and I were in Cittàgazze, and the Spectres killed him. It's what happens there.

PRESIDENT To what do you attribute your own survival?

MRS COULTER The power of prayer.

PRESIDENT You've offered to brief us on Lord Asriel's plans. In fact, we know them all. But there is one important question still outstanding.

MRS COULTER Which is?

PRESIDENT Where's your daughter?

MRS COULTER I've no idea. Why don't you ask the alethiometer?

The President glances at Brother Jasper.

BR JASPER I have done so. But the answer is too obscure for me to read.

MRS COULTER *(to Brother Jasper)* Well, once you've worked out what it's saying, I beg you to tell me. I'm Lyra's mother. I have the right to know.

PRESIDENT We would be more impressed by your maternal feelings, if you hadn't misused them so atrociously!

MRS COULTER What?

The President gets increasingly angry.

PRESIDENT You persuaded me to let you search for Lyra. I made *one* condition. You were to tell us when you had found her. You disobeyed. You hid her in a cave. You forced me to send the flower of the Church's youth in her pursuit, and many of them died. What was your motive? Were you protecting her? If so, from what?

Mrs Coulter loses control.

MRS COULTER From a body of men with a feverish obsession with sex, that's what.

PRESIDENT I beg your pardon?

MRS COULTER You heard me. Men whose furtive imaginations would crawl over my daughter like cockroaches. Men reeking of ancient sweat!

PRESIDENT You have one last chance to save yourself. Lord Asriel plans to kill the Authority. Does that appal you? Does it fill you with horror and fear?

MRS COULTER I think, what does it matter? The Authority's useless. Nobody sees him. Nobody hears him. Nobody cares what he thinks. The wicked get rich, and the poor and humble die in their millions without so much as a squeak of protest. *If* he's alive, he's clearly too old and decrepit to think or to act or even die. Wouldn't it be the kindest gesture, to seek him out and give him the gift of death?

PRESIDENT 'Out of their own mouths they shall condemn themselves.' Goodnight.

He and Brother Jasper leave.

MRS COULTER Oh, that was *stupid*!

We follow the President and Brother Jasper.

PRESIDENT It is imperative that we find the child. Has the alethiometer told you nothing?

BR JASPER That is *exactly* what it has told me, Father President. Nothing. Emptiness. An all-extending, malevolent grey. I simply can't work out what world it is trying to describe.

PRESIDENT You will continue your enquiries. As for the woman, she will die tomorrow. I fear confession will be of little advantage to her, but we must do what we can. Return to her cell after the Council of War, and hear her final words.

BR JASPER But Father President, the lady will be in bed. Father President?

Scene 6

Outskirts of the land of the dead. *The sound of seabirds. Ghosts are arriving. Lyra, Will and Pantalaimon arrive. An official – Mr Perkins – is there at a desk. He has a clipboard.*

PERKINS Excuse me! You people are still alive.

He prepares papers for them.

You wouldn't believe the number of living people they're sending us these days. Take these papers through to the holding area … make yourselves known … and wait.

LYRA How long for?

PERKINS Until you die, of course.

WILL And then what happens?

PERKINS Then you'll be travelling on by boat.

WILL Where to?

PERKINS I'm not permitted to tell you that. Proceed down there, first gate on the left.

To an anonymous queue waiting for attention:

Move on. Who's next?

Facetious:

Look alive!

Will and Lyra walk away.

WILL Do you reckon this is it?

LYRA It en't what I saw in my dream. It's more like a transit place.

WILL Papers! Look at 'em. They're just pages torn out of an exercise book.

LYRA At least he didn't look dangerous.

PANTALAIMON *All* of it's dangerous. Let's go back. I wanna go back.

LYRA Ssh …!

She calls:

Hello?

A man – Jeptha Jones – is there.

Is this all right? We was told to come in. I'm Lyra and this is Will. And this is my daemon, Pantalaimon.

Jeptha looks at them, puzzled.

JEPTHA You haven't brought your deaths with you.

LYRA Our *deaths*?

WILL No, we haven't. ***(quietly to Lyra)*** What's he talkin' about?

LYRA Dunno.

They follow Jeptha to where his family is sitting on camping chairs: his wife Hannah, old Mother Jones, her Death and a young boy.

We're sorry we've come without our deaths, if that's the normal way of things. But we hope you can help us. We're looking for the land of the dead, and we don't know how to get there. So if you can tell us about it, we'll be really grateful.

JEPTHA Come and sit down.

LYRA/WILL Thank you very much.

JEPTHA I'm Jeptha Jones. Hannah, I think they're hungry.

They come to the fire. Hannah pours soup into mugs for them.

LYRA Excuse me for asking, but are you dead?

JEPTHA ***(a bit hurt)*** Certainly not. Do you think we look it?

HANNAH We're still alive, like you. We're waiting here until our deaths tell us it's time to go.

LYRA Where are they?

HANNAH They're there.

She indicates a little group of anonymous figures sitting apart from them.

They don't bother us much. They keep themselves to themselves.

JEPTHA Except for our gran's.

Old Mother Jones's Death, who is as old as the gran, looks up.

Hello, old pal. Giving her a nice cuppa soup, are you?

Mother Jones's Death nods.

MOTHER JONES'S DEATH I am, I am.

JEPTHA *(to Lyra)* Before we arrived, we never could see our Deaths. We always had them, though, like everyone else.

LYRA What, all the time?

HANNAH Oh yes. Your Death comes into the world with you the minute you're born, and it stays with you every minute of your days, until it's time to go. It could come at any moment. When you're sick with a fever, or you choke on a piece of dry bread, or you stand at the top of a high building. In the middle of all your pain and hardship, your death comes to you kindly and says … 'Easy now, easy, child, you come along o' me.' And then it shows you into a boat, and out you sail.

LYRA Where to?

HANNAH Nobody knows.

LYRA If I want to get on to that boat … how can I find it?

HANNAH You must call up your Death.

LYRA *(frightened)* Will I see it? See it in front of me?

HANNAH It's the only way. *He'll* tell you.

They look at Mother Jones's Death. He chuckles.

MOTHER JONES'S DEATH I've heard of people like you, my gal. You don't want to know about your Deaths. That's why we stay out of sight. It's our good manners. But we're always there. You turn your head, and we dodge behind you. We can hide in a teacup, or a dewdrop, or in a breath of wind. But we get a bit bolder once your time comes near.

He pinches Mother Jones's cheek.

I never stray far from you these days, do I, sweetie?

LYRA What do I do, to call up my Death?

MOTHER JONES'S DEATH Just wish.

PANTALAIMON Don't. Don't!

LYRA I'm wishing.

They all look round.

JEPTHA Nothing.

HANNAH Just as well, eh? A child like her. Drink your soup.

They drink soup.

JEPTHA It's strange you got here. How did it happen?

LYRA Well, my mum and dad was a king and a queen … and they were thrown in prison …

HANNAH So you're a princess?

LYRA … and they shimmied down a rope. With me in their arms, 'cause I was just a baby. We was attacked by outlaws, and they would've roasted and eaten me, except I was rescued by Will. He'd fallen off the side of a ship, and he was washed up on a desolate shore and suckled by wolves … An' then …

The actor playing Pantalaimon appears as Lyra's Death.

HANNAH That's him.

LYRA Are you my Death?

LYRA'S DEATH Yes, my dear.

LYRA But you're not gonna take me?

LYRA'S DEATH Don't you want me to? I thought you wished.

LYRA I did … but I don't want to die, not yet.

LYRA'S DEATH I can wait. You'll go to the land of the dead in your own good time. And when you do, instead of your daemon, you'll have another friend, a special, devoted friend, who you don't know at all. But I'll have been with you every moment of your life. I know you better than you do yourself.

LYRA You don't understand. I want to go there now … but I wanna come back.

LYRA'S DEATH Nobody's ever come back, not for many a year. Why should you be any different?

LYRA I had someone taken away from me.

WILL Me too.

LYRA'S DEATH Everyone wants to see those people who've gone before. And if that is truly what you want, then I can show you the way. But as for returning … there I can't help you. You must manage on your own. Do you still want to go?

LYRA Will?

WILL Let's do it.

HANNAH Good luck, dear.

JEPTHA Safe journey.

HANNAH Hope you find what you're looking for.

LYRA'S DEATH Follow me.

As they leave, ghosts and Deaths bid them goodbye:

Goodbye/Take care/I hope you know what you're doing.

Lyra and Will walk on and reach ***the shores of a lake.***

LYRA'S DEATH This is as far as I can take you. Wait here.

He disappears.

LYRA Listen.

A rowing boat is heard.

WILL It's the boat.

LYRA Will? You ready?

Pantalaimon howls.

LYRA Ssh, Pan.

The boat appears and comes to rest, rowed by a very old man.

WILL I'll go first.

PANTALAIMON No!

BOATMAN Not him.

LYRA Not who?

The boatman indicates Pantalaimon.

I can't leave Pantalaimon behind. I'll die!

BOATMAN Isn't that what you want?

Pantalaimon howls and whimpers.

WILL No, that's not fair. Her daemon is part of her. I don't have to leave part of myself behind.

BOATMAN You do, young man. The only difference is that she can see it and talk to it. You will lose something just as precious, and you'll miss it as much as she does.

LYRA How will I find him again?

BOATMAN You never will.

LYRA What if he waits for us here, and we come back this way?

BOATMAN You won't come back this way, nor any other.

LYRA Will?

WILL *(to the boatman)* You're wrong. We will come back. We'll be the first since nearly ever. So what's the point of splitting up people and their daemons for the sake of a stupid rule? Let him come with us, just this once.

BOATMAN 'Just this once!' If only you knew how often I've heard those words. How many people do you think I've taken across this lake? Millions. Millions, millions. There's not one of 'em does it gladly. They struggle, they cry, they try to bribe me, they threaten and fight. They say they're not really dead, that it's all a mistake. They tell me about the gold and silver they've scraped together, and their powerful friends, the King of this and the Duke of that. And they all of them say that, just this once, the rules have got to be changed. They soon find out there's only one rule that matters. That they're in my boat, and I'm rowing that boat to the land of the dead, and I'll be rowing those kings and dukes as well before they know it. They're just the same as everyone else that breathes. And so are you.

WILL Lyra!

Lyra embraces Pantalaimon.

LYRA Pan, I love you. If I have to spend the rest of my life finding you again, I will. But I can't go back. I can't. I'm gonna push you away now. I'm sorry.

She pushes Pantalaimon away and steps on to the boat. Will steps on after. Pantalaimon crouches, forlorn and desolate. The boatman pushes off and the boat moves away from the shore. Lyra and Pantalaimon feel the pain of separation. Lyra cries in agony.

LYRA Oh, Pan!

Scene 7

A message is heard and/or seen from Lord Roke.

LORD ROKE *Lord Roke reporting from Geneva. Information regarding Lyra, Will or the knife amounts to nil. Preparations for war continue apace. Mrs Coulter unfortunately blew her cover and is now under sentence of death. She awaits the arrival of the rescue party with impatience.*

*Geneva: **Mrs Coulter's cell.** Mrs Coulter is pacing up and down anxiously. Lord Roke appears in the window.*

LORD ROKE Mrs Coulter! Mrs Coulter! Brother Jasper is on his way to see you.

MRS COULTER What does he want?

LORD ROKE Who knows? But it's your last chance to find out anything useful, so do please give it your best shot.

There is a knock on the door.

MRS COULTER Ssh!

Lord Roke gets out of sight. Mrs Coulter stretches out on the bed. She yawns and replies as though awoken from a deep sleep:

Come in.

Brother Jasper comes in with the alethiometer.

BR JASPER Mrs Coulter! Forgive my awakening you so late at night. I bring you wonderful news. This medallion …

He removes it from around his neck.

… confers forgiveness for all crimes past and present. No one has greater need of it than you. I will give it to you, and you will die as pure as a newborn child, if you can help me find your daughter.

MRS COULTER Well, naturally, I accept. But how can I help?

BR JASPER Just tell me: who is Roger?

MRS COULTER *Roger?* He was a friend of Lyra's, when she lived in Oxford.

BR JASPER And where is he now?

MRS COULTER I'm not sure I know how to answer that. Why do you ask?

BR JASPER Because I don't understand what the alethiometer is trying to tell me. Lyra has gone to look for this Roger in a world of endless grey and misery. Tell me where he is, and then I shall know where Lyra is … and you will bask forever in the bliss of the holy vision.

MRS COULTER Roger isn't anywhere. He's dead.

Brother Jasper is appalled.

BR JASPER Dead? *Dead?* No, that's impossible. Death is a place of infinite light and joy. If that's not true, then *nothing* is true!

He falls to his knees in great distress.

Save me! Don't let me believe her!

Mrs Coulter's monkey daemon moves seductively towards Brother Jasper's daemon, who responds shyly.

MRS COULTER Oh, Jasper, don't be upset. The moment I saw you, I knew you were different from the others. You have the courage to doubt a little. You have a human heart. But you've forgotten something.

He moves to place the medallion round her neck, but hesitates before touching her. She takes it and puts it on. He stays where he is, uncomfortably close to her but unable to move away.

Just tell me this: where Lyra's gone, is the boy with the knife there too?

BR JASPER Yes.

MRS COULTER Can you follow them there?

BR JASPER No.

MRS COULTER And why do you want to kill her? What is her name?

Her monkey daemon embraces his daemon lovingly.

BR JASPER It's Eve. The woman who … tempted the man. When they embraced the … ways of the flesh … and fell.

MRS COULTER And then?

BR JASPER We lost our innocence. And then Dust entered the world, and we've been fighting it ever since.

MRS COULTER So Lyra and Will are Eve and Adam? And that's what it's all about? You're trying to stop them?

BR JASPER Yes! If Lyra falls, it will happen again. The Triumph of Dust.

Gunshots are heard from outside. Lord Roke appears.

LORD ROKE The rescue party's arrived!

The golden monkey fixes Brother Jasper's daemon in a grip, paralysing her. Mrs Coulter flings Brother Jasper away from her. He falls to the ground and writhes in pain. To Brother Jasper:

MRS COULTER They lied, little man! Death is emptiness. Blankness. Nothing.

Soldiers of Lord Asriel enter and hustle her to the door. Armed clerics enter and attack them. Lord Roke is wounded.

LORD ROKE Run, my lady! Don't wait for me! When you see Lord Asriel, tell him I stayed at my post!

Scene 8

The land of the dead. The boat pulls up at a jetty *and Will and Lyra climb out. Harsh bird-like cries are heard. The boatman rows away.*

LYRA Do you feel it, Will? A big empty space where your daemon was?

WILL It's worse than empty. It's like a fist punched through my ribs and pulled something out.

There's a door.

LYRA We can't stay here.

WILL Better go through.

A harpy – No-Name – appears.

NO-NAME You are alive! And so-o-o-o sad!

She laughs.

LYRA What's that?

WILL It's a harpy. I've seen 'em in books.

NO-NAME Your mother went mad! And you were so-o-o-o ashamed of her!

WILL Yeah, well you better be able to fight as well as scream, 'cause we're going through that door!

NO-NAME Will's mummy is having nightmares! She's all alone! Ha ha ha ha!

LYRA Let us through!

NO-NAME You weren't Roger's friend! You thought he was thick! You just wanted to see your daddy, and Roger died!

She shrieks with laughter.

LYRA Who are you? What's your name?

NO-NAME No-Name!

LYRA What do you want with us, No-Name?

NO-NAME What can you do for me?

LYRA We could tell you where we've been. You might be interested.

NO-NAME You mean, you'll tell me a story?

LYRA Yeah.

NO-NAME Tell me a story I like, and I might let you through.

LYRA All right. My mother and father were the Duke and Duchess of Abingdon, and they was as rich as anything. The king used to come and hunt tigers in our enormous forest. And …

No-Name launches herself at Lyra.

NO-NAME Liar! Lyra the liar, Lyra the liar, Lyra the liar!

Will extends the knife. The harpy swoops away.

LYRA What's happening, Will? Why can't I lie any more?

WILL Through here.

Will slices through the door. They run through it into ***a vast, grey plain****. The plain is peopled with ghosts: sitting, crouching, all grey and listless. Harpies stalk about, tormenting them.*

WILL Look!

LYRA It's the place in my dream.

WILL Are these the ghosts?

LYRA Yeah. This is everyone in all the worlds who ever died.

WILL So many kids. It's so sad.

LYRA Will … I just thought of something. When Mr Scoresby was flying me from Bolvangar, Serafina was talking about me, 'cause she thought I was asleep. There's a prophecy about me. I'm gonna do something special. Something to do with death. A nyal … A nyler …

WILL Annihilation. Making something into nothing.

LYRA That's what I'll do. I'm gonna finish off death for good. Not just Roger, not just your father. All of them, every one. We're gonna cut a window into the world outside, and let the ghosts go free. So you better make sure that the knife can get us out.

WILL I'll find some place where they aren't all staring at us.

He turns to go.

LYRA Will.

WILL What?

LYRA I'm glad we're here together.

WILL Yeah, me too.

He goes. Children approach Lyra.

1ST GHOST-CHILD You! You're a new kid aren't you?

2ND GHOST-CHILD Do you miss your daemon?

LYRA Yeah. But I'm getting him back.

1ST GHOST-CHILD Everyone thinks that when they've just arrived.

3RD GHOST-CHILD Don't get any better either.

2ND GHOST-CHILD We're always thinking about daemons, en't we?

1ST GHOST-CHILD Yeah, we sit and remember 'em all the time.

2ND GHOST-CHILD My daemon …

3RD GHOST-CHILD Yeah?

2ND GHOST-CHILD … he used to think he'd settle as a bird, but I hoped he wouldn't, 'cause I liked stroking his fur.

1ST GHOST-CHILD My daemon and me used to play hide-and-seek.

Other ghost-children join in:

GHOST-CHILDREN – Mine used to curl up in my hand and go to sleep.

– I hurt my eye and I couldn't see, and he guided me all the way home.

– Mine never wanted to settle, but I wanted to grow up, and we used to argue.

– My daemon said, 'I'm over and done with', then he went forever. Just dissolved in the air. Now I ain't got him no more. I don't know what's going to happen ever again.

– There ain't *nothing* going to happen.

– You don't know that!

– That boy and this girl came, didn't they?

– That's the first thing that's happened in years and years!

– Nobody knew that *that* was going to happen.

– Well, maybe it's all going to change now.

– Yes! P'raps it'll change.

Roger appears.

ROGER Lyra!

LYRA Rodge!

He runs to her.

ROGER You've come to get me. I knew you would. I been calling for you ever since I died.

The others was making fun of me every time, but I went on saying your name …

LYRA I heard you.

ROGER How? How did you hear me?

LYRA I dreamed about you. I tried to hug you, but my arms went right through the air …

She reaches for him. He steps back and the harpies chuckle maliciously.

ROGER You can't even touch a person here, it's a terrible place. There's nothing changes, it's just grey and hopeless, and them bird-things … they come up behind you, and they whisper all the bad things you ever did. All the greedy and 'orrible thoughts you ever had, they know them all. You can't get away from 'em.

LYRA Don't worry, Rodge. I'm getting you out of here. Will's got a knife. It cuts through anything. And …

ROGER Who's Will?

LYRA My friend.

ROGER Is he your best friend? Is he better than me?

LYRA Not better, Rodge. No one could be better than what you were. He's just … the best friend I can touch … or hug …

ROGER Tell me about it.

LYRA Won't it make you sad?

ROGER It might do … but at least it'll feel alive.

LYRA Well … Will's the best friend I can get into fights with. Or share an apple with, or race up a hill, or sit in the sun.

The ghost-children cluster nearer.

GHOST-CHILDREN – Tell us about it!

– Tell us about the world!

– We've half-forgotten it, miss!

– Tell us!

Lyra looks round: the children are clustered around her, listening.

LYRA I said 'fight', 'cause Roger and me used to fight the other kids in the Oxford clay-beds.

Roger smiles.

ROGER Yeah, we did.

LYRA There's a row of willow trees along the side of the river, with the leaves all silvery underneath. Even in summer, when it's boiling hot, it's shady down there, and the clay is all sloshy and wet, but dry on top, so you can take a big slab in your hand like this.

Roger shows them.

ROGER Like that!

LYRA And there's a million different smells there. Like smoke from where the bricks are burning …

ROGER … and the river all warm and mouldy …

LYRA … and the baked potatoes that the burners ate …

ROGER Yeah, horrible food they eat …

LYRA … and there'd be Roger, me, Simon Parslow …

ROGER That's my cousin …

LYRA … Hugh Lovett, the butler's son …

ROGER … and Dick Purser, who could spit the furthest.

The children laugh.

LYRA Then when the clay was all over us head to foot …

She continues. Meanwhile:

Another part of the land of the dead.
Will extends the knife into the air, looks for a snag. He finds one and tries to cut. There's a hideous, grating noise. Will is about to try again. Jopari appears.

JOPARI Do that once more, and the knife will break.

WILL Father!

JOPARI Will.

WILL Aren't you angry with me? I didn't do what you said.

JOPARI There's no time to talk. You've got to get out. There may be a cleft in the rocks above us, but it'll be a long and difficult climb to find it. Where's Lyra?

WILL How did you know about Lyra?

JOPARI I was a shaman, Will. And a father too. We know these things.

WILL Follow me.

They see Lyra, who is finishing her story. Grown-up ghosts are listening as well as children. No-Name and three other harpies listen on the perimeter.

LYRA … and washed … and scrubbed … and put into bed. And we'd none of us had a more beautiful day in all our lives.

ROGER That's how it was.

The children applaud quietly.

LYRA Here, No-Name, you enjoyed that. When I told you a story before, you flew at me.

NO-NAME Because it was lies! Lies and fantasies!

LYRA But now you was listening quietly. Why was that?

NO-NAME Because you spoke the truth.

2ND HARPY Because it was nourishing.

3RD HARPY Because it was feeding us. Because we didn't know that there was anything in the world but lies and wickedness.

4TH HARPY Because it brought us news of the wind and the sun and the rain.

NO-NAME But now we've read your thoughts. You plan to escape. And there'll be no more stories! Traitor!

The harpies scream and fly at Lyra, terrifying the ghosts. Will leaps in towards Lyra, brandishing the knife, and the harpies draw back, squawking menacingly.

LYRA Will! Will! Will! Cut the window!

WILL I can't! The knife won't work! We're stuck!

LYRA No!

The harpies scream in triumph.

NO-NAME We'll revenge ourselves! We made this place a wasteland. Now we'll make it hell!

3RD HARPY We'll hurt you!

4TH HARPY We'll defile you!

2ND HARPY We'll send you mad with fear!

NO-NAME We'll torture you every day until you tell us stories!

The harpies advance on Lyra and Will.

WILL Stop! We'll make a bargain. Show Lyra and me and all these ghosts, the way to climb out of this place into the open air. And then forever after … you'll have the right to lead every ghost who arrives, all the way through the land of the dead, from the landing-post to the world outside.

NO-NAME That's no bargain! What do we get in return?

LYRA I'll tell you. Every one of those ghosts will have a story. They'll have *true* stories to tell you about the things they saw and heard and loved in the life that they left behind. You can ask them about their lives. And they gotta tell you.

NO-NAME What if they won't? What if they lie? Can we torture them forever?

Lyra glances at Will, who nods discreetly.

LYRA That's fair. Now show us the way!

A ghost steps forward.

1ST GHOST Not so fast. What will happen to us outside?

Other ghosts join in anxiously:

2ND GHOST We'll never survive!

3RD GHOST We won't exist!

1ST GHOST We'll be better off down here.

3RD GHOST Tell us what to expect!

2ND GHOST We won't go one step until you tell us!

Jopari steps forward.

JOPARI Listen to me, all of you. We will dissolve, just like your daemons did when you died. But they're not *nothing*. They've gone into the wind and the trees and the earth and all the living things. That's what will happen to us, I swear to you. I promise you on my honour. We'll drift apart, but we'll be out in the open, part of everything that's alive. Well, what do you say?

No-Name spreads her wings.

NO-NAME Follow me!

She moves away. The ghosts follow. Jopari gestures to put his arm round Lyra as they go.

Scene 9

Geneva. ***Mrs Coulter's cell.*** *Brother Jasper is there, in despair. The President paces about in agitation.*

PRESIDENT No! No! Since Lyra is who we know she is, she might *escape* the Land of the Dead. It's even possible that she'll …

BR JASPER What, Father President?

PRESIDENT It's too horrible to contemplate. If she could *free* the dead … if she could bring them into the world outside …

Voices are heard approaching.

1ST CLERIC He's here! He's with Brother Jasper!

2ND CLERIC Tell him the news!

3RD CLERIC Father President!

PRESIDENT Who's calling?

Clerics come in, armed for battle.

1ST CLERIC A miracle has happened! The Clouded Mountain has appeared!

All but the President fall to their knees.

PRESIDENT Who saw it?

3RD CLERIC I did, your Holiness. Like an enormous bank of clouds … sailing across the sky towards Lord Asriel's fortress … with cannons pointing out from the turrets, and lightning flashing and angels …!

PRESIDENT Angels!

3RD CLERIC … loyal angels, whirling and swooping around like a million birds.

PRESIDENT The Authority is advancing! Is this not the sternest rebuke to those who claimed he was feeble or sick or dead? He is alive! He commands his troops. He wields the sword of retribution! Praise be!

CLERICS Praise be!

PRESIDENT Prepare to support him on the ground. The power of righteousness be with you all. Go!

They start to go. Brother Jasper stays.

BR JASPER Father President, let me speak. I have sinned. I had evil thoughts.

PRESIDENT You are not the first young man to have been corrupted by Mrs Coulter. Make up for it on the battlefield.

BR JASPER No!

PRESIDENT Do you refuse me?

BR JASPER There's something else that I can do. A task far greater than anything that our army can accomplish. They won't find Lyra. She's escaped us over and over. The knife can cut her into any one of a million worlds. But I've got this.

He produces the alethiometer.

It will guide me to her, swift as the arrow of God. Wherever she's gone, wherever the boy can lead her. I'll strike her down, like the angel that blasted the Assyrians. Give me your blessing. Let me go.

An armed cleric appears at the door.

CLERIC Father President, the Council is assembled.

PRESIDENT Give me that.

He takes the cleric's sword, and gives it to Brother Jasper.

PRESIDENT Brother Jasper, you will be our ultimate guarantee that however this war will be decided, the infernal powers will not prevail. Find Lyra and kill her.

BR JASPER Thank you.

PRESIDENT I thank *you*. How much better it would be for us all if there had been a Brother Jasper in the Garden of Eden! We would never have left paradise.

They go.

Scene 10

A faltering message is seen/heard from Lord Roke.

LORD ROKE *Roke here ... gravest danger ... Lyra and Will are expected to leave the dead zone ... the assassin will find them once they have entered the living world ... the Clouded Mountain has set forth and will be visible from your fortress shortly ... on a personal note, regret return impossible ... I am proud to have served your lordship ... losing the light ...*

The land of the dead. *No-Name flies ahead. Lyra, Will and Roger follow her lead, at the head of a winding trail of ghosts.*

LYRA Is it much further, No-Name?

NO-NAME Just follow. If you can't see, listen. If you can't hear, feel.

The abyss appears.

WILL Lyra! Look at that.

LYRA What is it?

JOPARI It's the darkest secret of the underworld. When the first rebellion of the angels was defeated, the Authority sentenced its leader to something worse than death. He opened up this endless abyss and cast him into it, to fall for eternity. Ever since then, the abyss has continued its evil work.

Golden light appears, streaming downwards.

Do you see that golden light? It's Dust from all the worlds, being sucked into blackness and lost forever.

Will and Lyra look down it.

LYRA Can you see to the bottom, Will?

WILL Looks like it goes down forever. I don't like it. Something bad's gonna happen.

Lyra moves nearer to the edge.

JOPARI Careful, Lyra! If you fall, you'll fall for the rest of your life.

LYRA That wouldn't be long, though, would it? 'Cause I'd die of starvation.

She stands precariously on the edge. The ghosts call out to her to be careful.

LYRA Remember, Rodge, how you an' me used to climb on the roof at Jordan? And I dared you to stand on the top of a drainpipe, an' you …

She slips and falls into the abyss. The ghosts scream in terror, and:

WILL Lyra!

NO-NAME Make way!

No-Name spreads her wings, flies down towards Lyra and lifts her back to safety.

LYRA Oh, No-Name! Thank you! Thank you!

Roger calls.

ROGER Lyra! Look up there! There's daylight!

There's a ripple of excitement from the ghosts, as they all climb on.

Scene 11

Lord Asriel's fortress. Officers are looking out from the ramparts.

1ST OFFICER It's there! The Clouded Mountain!

2ND OFFICER It's getting closer!

3RD OFFICER Sound the alarm!

Lord Asriel appears below.

LORD ASRIEL Are our troops on the ground in place?

4TH OFFICER They are, my lord.

LORD ASRIEL And the angel battalions?

5TH OFFICER They're standing by.

Officers cross the battlefield from left and right, calling.

OFFICERS Stand by for the signal!/Get ready!/Sound the alert!

Mrs Coulter appears.

MRS COULTER Asriel!

LORD ASRIEL Quick, tell me. What have you learned?

MRS COULTER Her name is Eve.

LORD ASRIEL *Eve?* Then you were right, Marisa. She *is* unique. If she survives what lies ahead of her, she'll do all that I hoped to do myself. She'll smash the universe to pieces and she'll put it together in her *own* way.

4TH OFFICER My lord, it's gathering speed. Will you give the order?

LORD ASRIEL Let it come closer.

They look up at the Clouded Mountain.

Somewhere inside that terrifying mass is a crystal casket. And there the Authority lies. The angel-tyrant that I've sworn to destroy. And I don't have the knife, and I doubt that I ever shall. But there's something we possess that is just as powerful. It's this.

He touches her.

Our flesh. The angels long to have bodies like ours, so real, so strong, so firmly planted on the good earth. And if we *use* that power, if we're determined, we can brush them away like smoke!

He turns to the army around him:

Friends! This is the last rebellion and the best. Never before have angels, and humans, and beings from all the worlds and the power of nature itself, made common cause to build a world where there aren't any kingdoms at all. No kings, no bishops, no priests. We'll be free citizens of the republic of heaven.

He gives the signal.

Scene 12

The mouth of the land of the dead. *No-Name looks out. Lyra and Will look out after her.*

WILL Just breathe.

LYRA Amazing.

NO-NAME Have you no thanks for me?

LYRA Yeah, I do. You saved my life. And you brought us here, and you'll bring the ghosts up here for ever after. And if you en't got a name, that can't be right for a job that's so important. Iorek Byrnison called me 'Lyra Silvertongue' … and I'm giving a name to you. I'll call you 'Gracious Wings'.

NO-NAME I will see you again, Lyra Silvertongue.

LYRA And when you do, Gracious Wings, I won't be afraid. Goodbye.

She kisses No-Name. No-Name goes back into the land of the dead. Roger comes out, calling to the ghosts behind him.

ROGER I wanna go first. The rest of you, wait your turn.

To Lyra:

It will be all right, won't it?

LYRA Yeah.

ROGER I'll be part of the wind and the sun, just like Will's dad was saying?

LYRA I'm sure of it, Rodge. And when I die, I'll be a part of it with you.

ROGER That's good. That's *wonderful*, Lyra.

To the ghosts behind him:

Come on!

He disappears along with other ghosts beside him. Jopari appears.

JOPARI In a moment, Will, you'll go through to the battlefield. But there's something that I must say to you first, and Lyra too. When I left my world, I was as healthy and strong as a man could be. Twelve years later I was dying. Do you understand what that means? We can only survive in the world that we're born in. Lord Asriel's war will fail for the same reason. We must build the republic of heaven where we are. Because for us, there's no elsewhere.

WILL I've got something to say to you too. You said I was a warrior. You said it was in my nature, and I shouldn't argue. Well, you were wrong. My nature's what it is, and maybe I can't change that. But I can choose what I do. And I will.

JOPARI Well done, my son. I'm proud of you. No one on earth could have done better than this. Now go. Cut your window.

He disappears. Will cuts a window into . . .

*. . . **the battlefield.** Immediate noise and confusion. Fighters from both sides advance and retreat. Brother Jasper is seen with his sword drawn, stalking through the mêlée. Iorek appears and attacks him. Jasper's quickness and agility in the fight make Iorek look slow and clumsy. Brother Jasper wounds Iorek, and runs out of sight. Lyra and Will run on.*

LYRA Iorek!

IOREK Lyra Silvertongue! And Will!

LYRA You're wounded!

IOREK It was the priest. Get away from the battlefield. Leave at once. He's come to kill you.

WILL He can't do a thing. I've got the knife.

IOREK He has the symbol-reader, Will! He can outwit the knife! He even outwitted me. Run, quick as you can!

WILL You don't understand. I've got to find Lord Asriel, like I promised!

IOREK Then you must keep your promise. I'll find the priest, and do what I can to hold him back. If I survive, you children will always be welcome at Svalbard.

LYRA Won't you go back to the mountains?

IOREK No, my child. I was mistaken. My bears can't live in those snows. We must return to my ruined kingdom, and make what lives we can. Go well.

LYRA Go well, King Iorek.

Iorek cuffs Will gently and goes.

WILL Come on, let's go.

Lyra sees the Authority's crystal casket, lying where it fell on the battlefield.

LYRA Hang on. What's that?

WILL Dunno.

LYRA Let's go and look.

WILL Lyra!

LYRA It won't take a minute.

She goes and looks into it.

Will! There's a man inside.

Will goes and looks.

WILL That isn't a man. He's an angel, like Baruch and Balthamos, only … incredibly old.

LYRA I never seen anyone so old.

WILL He looks like one more breath'd be too much effort.

LYRA Look how he's scrabbling his fingers.

WILL He's crying.

LYRA It's horrible Can't we do summing to help him?

WILL Yeah, 'course we can. I'll cut him out.

He cuts the casket open and reaches in to lift the Authority out.

LYRA Don't touch him!

WILL Why?

LYRA 'Cause something's happening.

WILL Yeah! It is!

LYRA You opened the top, an' the air rushed in an' touched his face an' …

WILL He's getting fainter.

LYRA Like smoke.

WILL Like smoke dissolving.

LYRA He's smiling, look.

WILL He is!

LYRA 'Cause he's so glad to be dying! I can still see him a bit, can you?

WILL Yeah, just a flicker.

They watch.

Still smiling.

They watch.

LYRA He's gone.

Will starts to go.

WILL We can't hang about.

LYRA No, not if that priest is after us.

WILL Not just that! I gotta take this knife to your dad, so he can kill the Authority!

LYRA You're right. Let's go.

They go. Soldiers of Lord Asriel's army run on.

SOLDIERS I saw it!/Over here!/Lord Asriel!/It's the crystal casket!/It's the Authority!

Lord Asriel appears, his sword drawn.

LORD ASRIEL How did it happen?

1ST SOLDIER I saw it all, my lord. The Clouded Mountain sounded the retreat. I looked up, and there were four enemy angels flying away from it with something sparkling in their hands. The rebels attacked them, and it fell to earth. The Authority's there, inside that casket.

Lord Asriel goes to the casket and looks into it.

LORD ASRIEL It's empty.

SOLDIERS It can't be!/It was locked!/We saw him!

Serafina appears.

SERAFINA The children have freed him. But they're still on the battlefield and their assassin has nearly found them. Lord Asriel, you know what you have to do. I beg you, do it. All, all depends on the next few moments.

Mrs Coulter is heard calling.

MRS COULTER Asriel!

SERAFINA It's the woman who killed my witches. If I see her, I won't be able to let her live. Farewell.

She goes.

LORD ASRIEL Go, all of you.

The soldiers go. Mrs Coulter appears.

MRS COULTER Have you seen Lyra?

LORD ASRIEL She's very near. So is your little priest. You must stop him, Marisa. You're the only person who can do it. Lyra must live. That's all that matters.

MRS COULTER What about your republic?

LORD ASRIEL It's here! It's now! The knife did what it was meant to do, and the Authority's gone. But there's only one reason for my republic to exist. It's to prepare the world for Lyra.

MRS COULTER So we must save her at the cost of everything? Even our lives?

LORD ASRIEL Those most of all.

MRS COULTER So … just as Adam and Eve replenished the world with Dust … our children will do the same, in whatever Garden of Eden they find. And if they can't …

LORD ASRIEL … then it isn't our world to worry about. Our part is over.

The abyss appears.

MRS COULTER What is it?

LORD ASRIEL It's the end I dreamed of. It's the abyss.

Will is heard calling.

WILL Lord Asriel!

LORD ASRIEL Don't let them see you.

MRS COULTER But she must know what we're doing!

LORD ASRIEL No! She'd feel a burden of guilt at the very moment when she needs to be free. When she's older, she'll look back at it all. And then she'll know. Stand back.

They do. Will comes running on full-tilt. Lyra follows him.

WILL Lord Asriel! *(to Lyra)* He must be somewhere!

LYRA He'd find us, wouldn't he, if he wanted to? So would my mum. And listen. It's all gone quiet. The battle's over.

Mrs Coulter is about to speak. Asriel signals to her to be quiet. Unseen by the others, Brother Jasper appears, his sword raised.

LYRA Everyone's gone. Your dad. Serafina. Iorek, so old and powerless. It's all coming on to us now.

WILL Yeah … we gotta look after ourselves.

LYRA And find some place where we can't get killed.

WILL I'll cut a window.

He does. Brother Jasper is about to attack. Unseen by Lyra and Will, Mrs Coulter steps forward where Jasper can see her. She whispers fiercely:

MRS COULTER Jasper!

He stares at her. Lyra and Will go through the window and it closes behind them. Brother Jasper laughs.

BR JASPER They won't get away! There are windows everywhere. I know them all.

MRS COULTER Jasper, look at me. What do you see?

BR JASPER Sin. Corruption.

MRS COULTER Touch it. You wanted to, from the moment you saw me.

She kisses him. Unseen by Brother Jasper, Lord Asriel moves towards them.

Come with me, and you can touch it until you die. We'll fall forever, like the brightest and best of angels.

He pulls away from her.

BR JASPER No.

Lord Asriel seizes his hand. Mrs Coulter seizes the other.

No! No!

They struggle and fight. Stelmaria and the golden monkey throw themselves onto Brother Jasper, and all fall into the abyss.

Scene 13

An unknown world.

Lyra and Will are sitting on the ground. A bowl of hedge-fruit is between them. Lyra picks one up.

LYRA It's true what Roger said. You know at once when you like somebody. And I liked you.

WILL That night on the mountain … you were asleep … and I said to Pan that you were the best friend I'd ever had.

LYRA I heard you. I was lying awake!

WILL That's funny. 'Cause when Serafina was talking about the blackberries, I was lying awake as well.

LYRA When you said that to Pan, I wanted to sit up and say all the same things to you. Then your father died, because he wouldn't be unfaithful to your mother. You'd be like that.

She crushes a blackberry against his mouth.

I love you, Will.

They kiss.

Scene 14

***In an unknown world.** Serafina looks through her amber spyglass.*

SERAFINA The moon is high. But the clouds are still. Two children are lying in each other's arms in an unknown world. I look through the amber spyglass and I see a change. Dust is moving differently … there's a current here, a swirl of it there … all falling like rain on the poor parched throat of the earth. Life has returned. The world is renewed. The Dust pouring down from the stars has found its living home … and those two young children … no longer children … have made it happen.

Scene 15

***Same world.** Morning. Will and Lyra are asleep, their arms around each other. Pantalaimon and Will's daemon, Kirjava, are there, both as cats. Lyra wakes and sees them.*

LYRA Pan! Oh, Pan, you're back!

PANTALAIMON I thought I'd never, ever find you.

Lyra embraces him. Will wakes up and sees Kirjava.

WILL Hey, what's this?

PANTALAIMON What does it look like?

WILL Is it my daemon? Is it? Honest?

KIRJAVA Pick me up.

Will does.

WILL Hello.

KIRJAVA Hello.

WILL I'll have to give her a name.

Serafina is there.

SERAFINA I've done that already.

KIRJAVA My name is Kirjava.

SERAFINA Her shape has settled, I think.

LYRA And Pan?

PANTALAIMON I've settled too.

LYRA You're so beautiful. I can't believe that I got so used to being without you.

SERAFINA What you did, without knowing it, was what we witches have always done. It's painful for us, but once that's over, we and our daemons can wander free. So can you. You will always be one whole being, even when you are apart.

The daemons spring from Lyra's and Will's arms and crouch sadly at a distance from them.

LYRA Then why are they suddenly so sad?

SERAFINA Because they know what I have to tell you.

LYRA What?

SERAFINA The worlds were dying. Dust was flowing away, sucked in by that great abyss in the underworld. Only you could save it.

To Lyra:

This was your destiny, Lyra. To be true to your secret name. You were tempted and fell, and so the Triumph of Dust began. But it isn't complete. Dust continues to flow away, and all that is good will die unless you stop it.

LYRA *How* is it flowing?

WILL I think I know.

SERAFINA Dust escapes every time a window is left open, as though from a wound that goes on bleeding.

WILL You mean that the windows must all be closed?

SERAFINA They will be. It's a task for the angels.

WILL Then Lyra and me, we just gotta close our windows after we've made them. That'll be all right, won't it?

SERAFINA No. Every time you cut a window, it makes a Spectre. That's why Cittàgazze was so full of Spectres, because there are so many windows there.

LYRA We can't make Spectres, Will. We gotta cut no more windows.

WILL But Lyra and me are from different worlds. If I can't cut a window, then we …

He realises what he's saying.

… then we won't ever see each other. There's got to be *one*.

SERAFINA One is allowed.

WILL For us?

LYRA No. Not for us. It's for the dead to escape by, isn't it? We can't take that away from them.

WILL No, we can't.

LYRA But that don't matter. You and me can live in the same world, Will! It'll have to be yours, 'cause you can't leave your mother. But I got nobody now. I'll live with you.

WILL No! Don't you remember what my dad said? 'We can only survive in the world that we're born in.' That's why he was dying.

LYRA I don't care. I'll be happy to die, just so long as we're together.

WILL Do you think I could bear that? To see you getting sicker and sicker, while I got stronger and more grown-up every day? Do you think I could live on after you died? No, never, never.

LYRA We can't leave each other, Will. There must be a way! I know! I'll ask the alethiometer. It's bound to know.

She turns the wheels. Stares at it.

It isn't working. What's the matter with it?

SERAFINA Nothing's the matter. You've lost the child-like grace that made you able to read it. And you'll never be able to read it again in the way you did. But there's a different grace that comes with study. Work hard, and the time will come when you read it more deeply than ever. Will, you and Lyra must go into your world now. There'll be an angel there, who you must teach to close the windows. Then you will cut your final window. You and Lyra will say farewell. Then you must break the knife.

***The Botanic Gardens** in Will's world. Kirjava has stayed behind with Serafina.*

LYRA I want to kiss you and lie down with you … and sleep … and wake up with you every day of my life until I die.

WILL I'll always love you. And when I die, I'll drift about forever, all my atoms, till they mix with yours.

LYRA Every atom of you, every atom of me.

Pause.

WILL It's time.

LYRA Come on, Pan.

She picks up Pantalaimon.

If we meet someone that we like, later on, we gotta be good to them, and not make comparisons. But … once a year … just once a year … we could both come here, to the Botanic Gardens, on Midsummer night at midnight, … and talk till dawn, just like now, as though we were together again. Because we *will* be.

WILL I will. I promise. Wherever I am in the world, I'll come back here.

LYRA At midnight.

WILL Till the following dawn.

LYRA For as long as I live.

WILL For as long as I live.

He cuts a window.

LYRA Goodbye.

WILL Goodbye.

Lyra goes through. They stand looking at each other. Balthamos is there.

BALTHAMOS Now you must close it.

LYRA Close it.

Will closes the window. Lyra turns away in tears.

BALTHAMOS It will be the work of a lifetime to close them all. But one must do what's right, even after you have lost the one you love. Now break the knife.

Will extends the knife into the air.

WILL How?

BALTHAMOS Do as you did before. Think of whatever is most important to you. Then try to cut.

WILL Lyra.

The knife shatters. Dawn breaks: we're in the present day.

I wanted to go through after you.

LYRA I wanted to stay.

WILL But then I remembered what my dad said. There's no elsewhere …

LYRA You must be where you are …

WILL … and where you are is the place that matters most of all …

LYRA … 'cause it's the only place where you can make …

WILL … where you can build …

LYRA … where you can share …

WILL … what you've been looking for all along.

LYRA The Republic of Heaven.

Two clocks are heard striking. Lyra picks up Pantalaimon. She and Will pass each other and walk out of sight.

Introduction to the Activities

The activities and approaches will help you come to a greater understanding of the textual features and dramatic structures in *His Dark Materials*. They explore the writing process, style and writer's technique as well as the thematic, content-based issues and ideas. You will develop your analytical skills as well as the capacity to apply this critical thinking to other texts, ideas or issues.

The active nature of the activities and the critical thinking developed demand that you explore and respond to the play both in relation to its staging and performance, as well as in relation to the original Philip Pullman novels from which they have been adapted. Exploring and analysing the adaptation process allows you to examine the decisions, techniques and imagination required to move it from prose to script and from page to stage.

It is intended that, rather than working independently, you will collaborate in pairs and groups throughout under the guidance of your teacher. It is important that you are aware of the learning process and understand the aims and objectives of each session. Recording your thinking will help to inform the work and written responses as they develop.

From the initial planning to the final staging and performance of the play, the activities described can become an important part of the performance process.

An understanding of the writer's techniques, adaptation, the decision-making process and the roles of the writer, playwright, director and audience has a direct impact on the way in which actors and non-actors can approach a performance of the script.

The activities offered here provide a structure, which enable you to build your learning and understanding. Although the approaches are related to specific scenes and aspects of the play, the conventions and techniques can clearly be used in relation to other aspects of the play and/or other texts.

Paul Bunyan and Ruth Moore

Activity 1: Introducing daemons

Learning outcomes

You will:

- identify the author's use of the daemons in *His Dark Materials*
- develop your understanding of symbolism
- describe and explain accurately
- listen to, organise and present ideas.

You will do this by exploring the ways in which animals are used symbolically in literature to represent certain characteristics. For example, foxes are often characterised as being cunning and devious.

1 As a class, read lines 101–118 from Part 1, Act One, Scene 4 (pages 22–23)

from	Lord Asriel	Let's start with daemons . . .
to	Lord Asriel	. . . And why, if we were separated, would we die?

2 Discuss what you have found out about daemons from this extract. Why might the different characters have different animals as their daemons? Why these particular animals?

3 In pairs, sit back to back. Decide who will be **A** and who will be **B**. Your teacher will give all **As** a picture of an animal (without **Bs** seeing it) and all **Bs** a pencil and a piece of paper.

4 If you are **Student A**, begin to describe the animal. Explain its characteristics rather than its appearance and be careful not to mention its name at any point. For example, when describing a bear you might say 'it is a strong, inquisitive animal'. **Student B** needs to decide which animal is being described and either produce a quick sketch of it or write down the name of that animal. Your teacher will stop you after a very short period of time, so the animal needs to be sketched or identified as quickly as possible.

5 When your teacher stops you, compare the drawing, or name written down, with the picture **Student A** was given. Do you have the same animal? If so, what part of the description helped you to arrive at this? If you have a different animal, what characteristics led you to this decision?

6 Move into a large circle and place all the pictures of the animals in the middle of the circle for everyone in the class to see.

7 After looking at all the animals, decide which daemon you would choose for yourself and explain why you have made that choice. What characteristics do you feel you have in common? You might also discuss what daemons you would choose for other people!

What have I learnt?

- What skills have you used/developed in this activity?
- What have you learnt about daemons in *His Dark Materials*?
- How did describing the animal help you to think about the use of symbolism?

Activity 2a: Setting a context and exploring the two worlds of Oxford

Learning outcomes

You will:

- analyse pictures
- investigate, in role, the context and setting of the play
- describe and explain accurately
- listen to and select information.

You will do this by exploring the two worlds of Oxford through a Guided Tour activity and feeding back what you have discovered about the two places.

1 Sit in a large semi-circle facing the projected images of the Oxford Botanic Gardens. (Alternatively, your teacher may hand out photocopies of the images.) One picture depicts Lyra's Oxford (1), with a signpost giving directions to Jordan College; the other picture depicts Will's Oxford (2). It is clear that the two pictures are of the same place but with some subtle differences.

2 Identify what you can see in the two pictures. First, describe what you actually see and then try to interpret the picture. For example, what sort of place is it? What are the differences between the two pictures?

3 Get into pairs, then decide who is **A** and who is **B**.

4 As a class, you are divided in half. All **Student A**s in one half of the class are given the picture of Lyra's Oxford (1), while all **Student A**s in the other half have Will's Oxford (2). If you are **Student A**, make sure you look carefully at the picture you have been given, as this is the place you are about to explore with your partner on a **Guided Tour**.

> **Guided Tour** in pairs, **A** (with eyes open) leads **B** (with eyes closed) slowly through an imaginary environment, while providing a spoken commentary. The environment or location may be based on text but will usually be stimulated by a printed or projected map or picture.

5 **Student A:** you need to imagine that you know the place very well and, using the picture, take your partner on a Guided Tour, describing and commenting on the things they can see around them as you move around the space.

Student B: you need to keep your eyes closed, while your partner holds you by the arm and guides you around the space. You need to listen to the description carefully as you will be asked later to feed back to the class what you have found out.

6 Your teacher may decide to play some music during this activity. If so, listen to it as you make your way around the place.

7 When you are asked to freeze, stop quickly and keep very still and silent.

8 Now it is time to feed back to the class. If you are **Student B**, describe to the class what you have seen with your 'drama eyes', heard with your 'drama ears' and perhaps smelt with your 'drama nose' as you were guided around 'Oxford'. Listen carefully to the information provided by the other students.

What have I learnt?

- What skills have you used/developed in this activity?
- How were you able to describe the place in such detail? What did you use to help you do this?
- What have you learnt about the setting and context of the play?

Activity 2b: Introducing the play and developing the context

Learning outcomes

You will:

- further investigate the context and setting of the play
- describe and explain accurately
- listen to and think carefully about the text you hear.

You will do this by continuing to explore the two worlds and being introduced to an extract from the play.

1 Reverse your roles from Activity 2a (page 285) by swapping the tasks of the **As** and **Bs** in your pair. This time, the **Bs** imagine that they know the place very well and take their partners on a Guided Tour.

2 Listen carefully to your teacher narrating information about the place, using information and ideas from the feedback that you have just given.

3 Remember that when you hear the word 'freeze', you must stop exactly where you are, stay completely still and listen to what is said.

4 Continue the Guided Tour. As well as listening carefully to the description and music (if music is being played), if you are **Student A** you can now ask **Student B** questions about the place.

5 Freeze and listen to the following extracts from the play and, if shown, follow the text projected onto a screen.

Extract 1: lines 332–343 from Part 1, Act Two, Scene 3 (pages 100–101)

from	LORD ASRIEL	There are as many worlds as there are possibilities.
to	LORD ASRIEL	I'm going to destroy it.

Extract 2: lines 53–63 from Part 1, Act Two, Scene 6 (pages 112–113)

from	SERAFINA	All across the North ...
to	SERAFINA	... till the prophecy has run its course.

What have I learnt?

- What else have you learnt about the setting and context of the play?
- By investigating the extracts, what other information have you gained?
- Which issues or ideas do you think will be particularly significant in the play?
- How has the Guided Tour activity helped you to gain an understanding of the setting and enabled you to think about the context of the play?

Activity 3: Role of Northern Lights: exploring the character of Lord Asriel

Learning outcomes

You will:

- investigate the character of Lord Asriel
- select appropriate information
- narrow down, organise and present ideas.

You will do this by analysing extracts from the play and making reasoned judgements about the information you are given.

1 As a class, read extracts 1–3. You can follow the text in your books or projected onto a screen.

Extract 1: lines 112–136 from Part 1, Act One, Scene 2 (pages 13–14)

from	FRA PAVEL	Why was I not informed of Lord Asriel's visit?
to	MASTER	I'll do as you say. But under protest.

Extract 2: lines 15–19 from Part 1, Act One, Scene 3 (page 15)

from	HOPCRAFT	Gentlemen, gentlemen! What's going on?
to	1ST SCHOLAR	Well, some of us do.

Extract 3: lines 113–225 from Part 1, Act One, Scene 4 (pages 23–27)

from	LORD ASRIEL	Yet a child's daemon can change whenever it wants to.
to	PRO	*What* did you say? *What did* you say? (etc)

2 As a class, sit in a large semi-circle facing the projected image of the Aurora Borealis (Northern Lights). On pieces of card are all the words that surround the alethiometer – the instrument given to Lyra to help her identify the truth – for example, perseverance, fear, natural wisdom, honesty, power.

3 Use the **Role on the Wall** convention to explore the character of Lord Asriel. To do this you need to identify from extracts 1–3 what you know about him. Then select words from the cards that you feel best describe him. Next, place the selected words on the image of the Northern Lights, thinking carefully about where you might put the word according to the colour beneath it.

> **Role on the Wall** to help define character traits at particular moments in a drama. Statements or words are positioned on a large outline of a particular character usually pinned on a wall or laid on the floor.

4 You will return to this Role on the Northern Lights throughout the scheme of work by adding words and discussing your previous choices at different stages. You might also want to record on the image your responses, ideas and comments about the play as a whole in the same way described above. This will provide a useful prompt and recap tool, and provide you with a valuable resource when you are planning your written responses to the text.

5 From the information you have gained so far, what daemon would you give to Lord Asriel if it were still able to change its form? Select a picture of an animal and place it on the Northern Lights image. Justify your choice to the rest of the class by providing a quotation from the text extracts.

What have I learnt?

- What analytical skills have you developed in this activity?
- How did you decide what words to choose for Lord Asriel? Do you think this description will remain throughout the whole play? Why?
- How does placing the words carefully on the different colours add to the meaning of those words?
- How might this activity help with your understanding of the writer's use of colour in the play (or novels) of *His Dark Materials*?

Activity 4a: Introducing and investigating the play – images of Lyra

Learning outcomes

You will:

- develop the use of space, facial expression, gesture and tone
- investigate and analyse the script
- question critically the images of Lyra.

You will do this by investigating the extracts and considering how the script might be staged in order to produce Digital Video Clips which present an image of Lyra.

1 Form groups of between 3 and 5 students. Each group will be given an extract from the play (see extracts 1–7 on page 291). Don't forget to look at the stage instructions before, during and after the lines of dialogue.

Extract 1: lines 176–233 from Part 1, Act One, Scene 5 (pages 34–36)

from	MASTER	One moment, Lyra.
to	LYRA	We're gonna rescue him. I swear it.

Extract 2: lines 1–53 from Part 1, Act One, Scene 7 (pages 39–42)

from	LYRA	I en't never been pretty before.
to	MRS COULTER	One can be better known than one is aware of.

Extract 3: lines 15–49 from Part 1, Act One, Scene 8 (pages 47–48)

from	FRA PAVEL	Lyra has run away.
to	FRA PAVEL	Wait in your study. You will shortly receive a visit.

Extract 4: lines 138–216 from Part 1, Act One, Scene 11 (pages 78–81)

from	DR SARGENT	Gentlemen, what very good timing.
to	MRS COULTER	He's Lord Asriel.

Extract 5: lines 1–63 from Part 1, Act Two, Scene 2 (pages 86–88)

from	SERAFINA	Are the children asleep down there?
to	SERAFINA	But if she acts in ignorance, out of her own true impulse, then she . . .

Extract 6: lines 46–86 from Part 1, Act Two, Scene 3 (pages 103–105)

from	LORD BOREAL	No, you may not.
to	FRA PAVEL	Seize her!

Extract 7: lines 68–121 from Part 1, Act Two, Scene 9 (pages 129–131)

from	WILL	I'm looking for my father.
to	WILL	I'll meet you back here.

2 In your group, produce a short **Digital Video Clip** of the extract you have been given. Begin with a **Still Picture**, followed by an **Action Reading** of the script and then **Freeze** at the end in a final Still Picture. You need to investigate the script and search for clues about the characters, story and setting in order to produce an accurate Action Reading of the extract.

Digital Video Clip a short, repeatable dramatic sequence is 'bookended' with a Still Picture at the start and a Still Picture at the end.

Still Image/Still Picture/Freeze-frame a still image is created by participants in the drama standing motionless, often at a given sign by your teacher or as a result of being sculpted by other students into the frozen image. This convention is used to mark a significant moment or enable time for reflection.

Action Reading students, in role, walk through a scene, speaking the lines and adding gestures and movements, while reading from scripts.

3 As a class, produce your Digital Video Clips as **Rolling Theatre**. Music could be used to guide you.

a All the groups freeze in their initial Still Picture.
b The first group unfreezes, adds the action, then freezes again. When they freeze, the next group know they can begin.
c This continues with all the groups producing their Digital Video Clip, until all groups have shown their pieces.

Rolling Theatre a means by which groups can share their work on different aspects of drama, learning from each other by running several rehearsed sections one after another.

When you are not presenting your Digital Video Clip, you can relax slightly in order to listen to and see the other groups. However, you must remain in your place in order for all the groups to freeze in their final Still Picture at the end.

What have I learnt?

- How did performing these extracts help you to gain an understanding of the issues, characters and setting?
- How did you use space, gestures, tone and facial expressions during the Digital Video Clip?
- What have you learnt about Lyra by listening to/watching the other groups?

Activity 4b: Images of Lyra

Learning outcomes

You will:

- develop the use of space, facial expression and gesture
- investigate and analyse the script, selecting relevant information and explore the use of stillness and silence in a production of the play
- explore a specific character and consider the actor's and playwright's response to the complexity of the role.

You will do this by producing a Still Picture that defines Lyra's character and by attributing a specific word to the image.

1 In the same groups as Activity 4a (page 290), use the extract you were given and the information gained from producing your Digital Video Clip to present a Still Picture that describes how Lyra is seen at this stage in the play. You can present an image of Lyra as seen by the other characters or one that suggests the audience's view of Lyra as she presents herself.

2 Choose a word from the alethiometer list to describe your image. Take the word, written on a piece of card, and place it in front of your Still Picture.

3 The class is divided in half. One half freeze in their chosen images, while the other half 'read' the images and words. Then swap roles.

4 Take up your positions in your group again, but this time the groups form a large circle with your teacher standing in the middle. Freeze in your Still Picture, which shows the image of Lyra. An image of the alethiometer is projected onto a screen and a large arrow shape is placed in the centre of the circle like a clock hand.

5 Decide where you think the arrow would point in terms of the 'truest' image of Lyra. Which image presents the 'truth' about her?

   a Move the arrow and justify your choice.
   b Further arrows are added to the circle.
   c Other students are asked whether they agree with your positioning and they move the arrows to where they feel they are best placed.

   The three arrows help you to explore the different aspects of Lyra's personality that make up her character.

6 Discuss the different aspects of people's characters and the complexity of developing that in a play or novel.

What have I learnt?

- What evidence did you use to decide on your Still Picture and the positioning of the arrow?
- How might the different aspects of Lyra's character be a problem and/or benefit to the playwright and actor?
- How did this activity help you to develop your understanding of Lyra's character?

Activity 5a: Sculpting the characters – Describing the Space and the motivation

Learning outcomes

You will:

- develop analytical skills
- investigate the motivation and thoughts of particular characters
- develop your understanding of the writer's techniques and intentions.

You will do this by analysing a specific scene in detail through the use of a number of drama conventions.

1 As a class, read lines 1–86 from Part 2, Act One, Scene 4 (pages 156–160)

from	LYRA	What do you think?
to	LORD BOREAL	Oh no. Although I'm sure she'll scream and shout and cause an appalling scene.

2 Your teacher selects four students to take the roles of Lord Boreal, Mrs Coulter, Lyra and Will.

3 The other students in the class **Sculpt** these four characters into the scene at this point in the play. You will need to consider their frozen positions, facial expressions, gestures.

> **Sculpting** participants offer suggestions to place an individual in a significant, frozen position so that an analysis can be made.

4 Your teacher stands between two of the characters and asks you to try to **Describe the Space** between the characters. You might suggest various options, for example, the space of unhappiness,

ignorance, anger. Using the alethiometer, identify a word that explains what motivates a specific character at this point in the play.

> **Describe/Name the Space** participants are invited to offer words to describe a physical (or metaphorical) space between two characters at a moment of tension in the drama. The same technique can be used to describe barriers that exist between characters and situations.

5 A further three students are selected to represent the daemons. The rest of the class Sculpt the three daemons into the frozen image at the same point in the scene. To do this you will need to present the daemons in such a way that they suggest certain characteristics or feelings, rather than presenting them as particular animals.

6 All the characters freeze, and the teacher reads lines 87–89

from	MRS COULTER	She'll learn to behave when I've got her under lock and key, I can assure you of that.
to	LYRA	*(to Will)* Bloody old cow.

What have I learnt?

- What helped you to Sculpt the characters and how did you decide on the positioning?
- How has this activity helped you to think about the different characters and the relationships between them?
- How could you use the sculpting of characters and daemons to influence how you might stage the play?

Activity 5b: The daemons speak the characters' thoughts

Learning outcomes

You will:

- explore the tension in the play
- make reasoned judgements and organise and present your ideas
- investigate and analyse the text to identify the character's thoughts and motivation.

You will do this by speaking the daemons' thoughts and revealing the tension in the scene and the motivation of the characters.

1 The characters and daemons remain sculpted in the scene from Activity 5a (page 295). The daemons are to speak the characters' thoughts, revealing the truth about what they are thinking at any point in the scene. For some, this may be exactly what they are saying but for others the thoughts may be very different from what we hear the characters say. Thoughts which are unconnected to the content of the scene, for example, thoughts about Roger, may also enter their heads.

2 The student playing Mrs Coulter reads lines 90–91 from Part 2, Act One, Scene 4 (page 160) 'I shall *never* forgive you for sending her into that terrible Spectre-world.'

- **a** What would Mrs Coulter be thinking at this point?
- **b** After your suggestions, her daemon selects one of them and says the line. Suggestions can also be given as to what the other characters are thinking.
- **c** The student playing Mrs Coulter repeats lines 90–91 from the script, then her daemon and one of the other daemons speaks the thoughts.

This process continues with a reading of the script and the daemons speaking the thoughts.

3 Once you have seen this process being modelled, move into a group of 5 to 7 to explore the scene yourselves in the same way. A different part of the scene is allocated to each group so that after a few minutes you can present your work through the Rolling Theatre technique described in Activity 4a (page 290).

What have I learnt?

- How does this activity help you to explore the tension in the scene?
- How might such an activity help the actors prepare for the staging of this particular scene?
- What skills did you use during the group activity and what helped you to decide on the daemons' thoughts?

Activity 5c: Exploring motivation in the scene – Action Narration

Learning outcomes

You will:

- analyse the motivation of the characters
- identify and refine the acting skills required to express the characters' motivation
- consider the roles of the playwright, actors and director.

You will do this by analysing extracts from the play and making reasoned judgements about the information you are given.

1 As a class, return to the sculpted characters from Activity 5a (page 295).

a Your teacher takes the place of Mrs Coulter and demonstrates the **Action Narration** convention by clapping her/his hands (directing that all the actors should freeze at that point) and then saying what the character is going to do next and why. For example, 'I am going to move towards Lord Boreal as I speak because I am annoyed by what he did to Lyra.'

b Your teacher then claps her/his hands again to indicate that the actors in role can come to life.

c Then your teacher, in role as Mrs Coulter, turns to Lord Boreal, looks annoyed and speaks the lines 90–91 from Part 2, Act One, Scene 4 (page 160) 'I shall *never* forgive you for sending her into that terrible Spectre-world.'

Action Narration a convention which requires each participant to pause and verbalise motives and descriptions of actions before they undertake them in an improvisation.

2 Your teacher then explains that each of the characters can clap her/his hands to freeze the action, allowing them to Action Narrate what they are going to do and/or say next and why. The aim is that no one moves or speaks without revealing their motives.

The Action Narrated scene continues until all the characters have revealed their motives for their actions and dialogue.

3 Once you have seen this process being modelled, move into a group of between 5 and 7 to explore the scene yourselves in the same way.

What have I learnt?

- What role does the playwright, actor or director have in revealing and/or deciding on the characters' motivation? How do they achieve this?
- How does this activity enable you to develop your understanding of the writer's techniques?
- What skills were required for you to complete the action narrated scene? How might these skills help your understanding of the play?

Activity 5d: Placing the text

Learning outcomes

You will:

- write for a specific audience, with a specific purpose
- select appropriate information from the text
- explore the themes and tensions in the play
- organise and present your ideas appropriately.

You will do this by producing and placing pieces of text into the scene and making a contribution to the drama.

1 As a class, return to the sculpted characters in Activity 5a (page 295). Now read lines 92–147 from Part 2, Act One, Scene 4 (pages 160–2)

from	LORD BOREAL	She's in no danger.
to	MRS COULTER	And what makes him so remarkable?

All the characters then freeze. At this stage, Lyra will be outside the scene but should be sculpted near to where you believe the window might be.

2 Your teacher holds up a blank piece of paper in various positions within the scene while asking what text you think would be on the piece of paper. Depending on where the piece of paper is positioned, you will make different suggestions as to what may appear on it. If it is placed in Lord Boreal's desk you might say it is an official document from the Church. Placed in one of Lyra's pockets or screwed up and thrown at her feet, you might suggest something different, such as a letter to her father or an extract from Will's father's research.

3 In pairs, create a piece of text, such as those suggested above, that could appear in any of the places in the scene. It is important that you create two identical versions of this piece of text.

4 When you have all completed the pieces of text, set up the sculpted characters again and, one by one, place one copy of the text where you think it would be found in the scene. You need to remember where you placed your text because you will be reading it out later when one of the characters identifies it.

- **a** Once all the pieces of text have been placed, the sculpted characters gradually come to life and turn to, look at and/or open the pieces of text, one at a time in turn.
- **b** As they come across each piece of text, they look at the text and freeze. If you placed this particular piece of text, you read it out, at this point, from the identical copy you have retained. (You need to think about how you will read the text out loud in terms of the tone, style and pace.)
- **c** The drama continues but stops at each piece of text while different students read them out, until all the pieces of text have been included. Music might be used to introduce and close the sequence.

What have I learnt?

- What skills did you need to produce a piece of text that could be placed in the scene?
- What helped you to decide how to read out your piece of text?
- How might this activity help you to explore the tensions and themes of the play?

Activity 6: Further exploration of the text – the significance of the knife

Learning outcomes

You will:

- develop the use of space, language, facial expression and gesture
- investigate and analyse the script, selecting relevant information to explore the significance of a knife in the play
- analyse and question critically others' performances
- deduce and predict what events and themes are important in the play.

You will do this by analysing extracts from the play and making reasoned judgements about the information you are given.

1 You will be working in a small group of between 3 and 5 students. As with the previous extracts exploring Lyra's character (see Activity 4a, page 290), each group has an extract from the play (see extracts 1–9 below).

Extract 1: line 45, Scene 12, to line 23, Scene 13, from Part 1, Act Two (pages 138–141)

from	WILL	Give it back to us.
to	PARADISI	Now it has passed to you.

Extract 2: lines 24–64 from Part 1, Act Two, Scene 13 (pages 141–143)

from	WILL	Look, the only reason I got mixed up in this . . .
to	PARADISI	And in the war that is to come, you may be called to aim it even higher.

Extract 3: lines 59–96 from Part 2, Act One, Scene 2 (pages 154–155)

from	HARDBALL CLERIC	But there's a knife this time.
to	WILY CLERIC	What would be wrong with that?

Extract 4: lines 1–35 from Part 2, Act One, Scene 4 (pages 156–157)

from	LYRA	What do you think?
to	LYRA	While I stay here?

Extract 5: lines 1–25 from Part 2, Act One, Scene 8 (pages 173–174)

from	SERAFINA	Stop! This is where we'll rest for the night.
to	WILL	. . . I think there's Spectres there as well.

Extract 6: lines 1–71 from Part 2, Act One, Scene 11 (pages 183–186)

from	JOPARI	Give me your hand.
to	WILL	Father?

Extract 7: lines 25–69 from Part 2, Act One, Scene 17 (pages 201–203)

from	WILL	I'll show you. I challenge you to fight me in single combat.
to	WILL	But first, I've got to rescue Lyra.

Extract 8: lines 90–109 from Part 2, Act One, Scene 19 (pages 210–211)

from	MRS COULTER	Asriel!
to	LORD ASRIEL	Lyra! Lyra!

Extract 9: lines 127–168 from Part 2, Act Two, Scene 2 (pages 219–220)

from	IOREK	Let me see it.
to	IOREK	I'll build a fire.

2 Produce a short Digital Video Clip of your extract. Begin with a Still Picture, followed by an Action Reading of the script and then Freeze at the end. To do this you will need to investigate the script and search for clues about the characters, story and setting. A symbolic knife will be given to your group, which should be included in your Digital Video Clip.

3 Instead of the extracts being presented as Rolling Theatre, this time you will use a slightly different technique.

- **a** All the knives are collected in from the groups.
- **b** All the groups freeze in the initial Still Pictures.
- **c** Your teacher moves to one group and places one of the knives in their scene, holding on to the remaining knives.
- **d** If this is your group, you unfreeze, add the action and then freeze again.
- **e** When you have frozen in your final image, take the knife to another group and place it in their scene. You then return to your own group and the next group knows they can begin.

This continues until all groups have shown their pieces. Music might be used.

4 When all the groups have shown their pieces and have frozen in the final image, a member of the final group brings the knife to your teacher and presents it to them.

Holding the knife, your teacher then reads lines 9–85 from Part 2, Act Two, Scene 4 (pages 228–231)

from	IOREK	What will you do with the knife?
to	WILL	Let's go.

Your teacher might choose to read instead an extract from Chapter 15 ('The Forge') from the novel *The Amber Spyglass* to develop a link with Activity 7 – exploring the adaptation process.

What have I learnt?

- What skills have you used/developed in this activity?
- What have you learnt about the significance of the knife? How does this relate to other ideas and events in *His Dark Materials*?
- Why is one knife, passed between the groups, used in the final activity, rather than a knife for each group? How might this decision to use one knife help your understanding of the writers' techniques in the novel and play?

Activity 7: From personal to universal – exploring the adaptation process

Learning outcomes

You will:

- analyse the decisions and techniques used during the adaptation process
- select, organise and present relevant information and ideas in script and performance
- develop analytical skills and explore the writer's intentions.

You will do this by analysing a specific aspect of the novel and how it might be adapted for the stage.

1. As a class, sit in a large semi-circle facing the projected text. Your teacher reads or plays a recording from Chapter 21 ('The Harpies') from the novel *The Amber Spyglass* (pages 294–300, from 'Then suddenly there was the boat' to '. . . each of them saw their own expression on the other's face').
2. Working in groups of between 3 and 5 students, each group is given a section of the extract that the teacher reads aloud. Think about how you could adapt this extract into a play. How will you use the description in the novel? What will you do about the boat? How will you present the daemons?
3. Create a script and produce an Action Reading of the play as it is to be acted. Once all the adaptations are complete, you can produce them as Rolling Theatre (described in Activity 4a, page 290).

What have I learnt?

- What do you feel influences the adaptation process in terms of the decisions you needed to make?
- How does having to adapt a scene yourself help you to analyse this particular scene in the play?
- What was the hardest part of the process? Why? What skills did this require?

Activity 8: Placing the Writer and the Reader

Learning outcomes

You will:

- analyse authorial intention and techniques, and explore the role of the reader and empathy in the text
- select and present evidence from the text to justify your comments
- listen with discrimination, weigh viewpoints and question critically.

You will do this by Placing the Writer and Reader in a particular scene in order to explore the intentions and techniques employed.

1 As a class, sit in a large circle. Return to page 298 in the novel *The Amber Spyglass*, the point at which Lyra pushes Pantalaimon away:

> I *swear* we're coming back – I will – take care, my dear – you'll be safe – we will come back, and if I have to spend every minute of my life finding you again I will, I won't stop, I won't rest, I won't – oh Pan – dear Pan – I've got to, I've got to . . .
>
> And she pushed him away, so that he crouched bitter and cold and frightened on the muddy ground.

2 A member of the class is given the role of Lyra. Using the space inside the circle, each student sculpts her into the position they believe she will be in when the action takes place. Students may question the positioning of others and will re-Sculpt Lyra into a position of their choosing.

3 Other members of the class are given the roles of Will, Pantalaimon and the boatman. These characters are sculpted by the rest of the class into the scene and all freeze while the following extract from page 298 is read.

> And she pushed him away, so that he crouched bitter and cold and frightened on the muddy ground.

What animal he was now, Will could hardly tell. He seemed to be so young, a cub, a puppy, something helpless and beaten, a creature so sunk in misery that it was more misery than creature.

4 Another member of the class is given the role of the 'writer' (Philip Pullman).

- **a** Position the writer in the frozen scene where you think he should be. You might use various criteria for this, including the writer's distance from certain characters, the empathy created, the events, the writer's intention and what control the narrator has.
- **b** Justify your choice, using evidence from the text to support your ideas.
- **c** Discuss the positioning as a class. Throughout this discussion, other students should demonstrate the position they feel is most appropriate by moving and Placing the Writer and justifying their choice.

> **Placing the Author** in order to help students to appreciate an author's perspective, a student or teacher represents the presence, at a defined moment in the drama, of the author.

5 Another member of the class is given the role of the 'reader'.

- **a** Position the reader in the frozen scene where you think s/he should be. You might use various criteria for this, including the reader's distance from certain characters, the empathy felt, the events and the reader's understanding of a particular idea.
- **b** Justify your choice, using evidence from the text to support your ideas.
- **c** As a class, discuss the positioning of the reader. Throughout this discussion, other students should demonstrate the position they feel is most appropriate by moving and Placing the reader and justifying their choice.

6 Try to Describe the Space between the reader and the writer.

What have I learnt?

- How does physically Placing the Writer and/or Reader help your understanding of the writer's perspective and techniques?
- What skills were required when deciding where to place the reader or writer and justifying your choice?
- How did the discussion and repositioning inform your understanding/thinking?
- How was empathy created in this extract? Why?

Activity 9: Placing the Playwright

Learning outcomes

You will:

- analyse the adaptation process and discuss the complex decisions that are involved
- analyse the playwright's intention and techniques, and explore the role of the audience in the play
- make decisions and select evidence to support your decisions and ideas.

You will do this by Placing the Playwright into the scene, and exploring the techniques he has used and the decisions he has made.

1 Read lines 145–190 (and all the stage instructions) from Part 2, Act Two, Scene 6 (pages 244–245)

from	WILL	I'll go first.
to	LYRA	I'm gonna push you away now. I'm sorry.

It is the same scene as the extracts from the novel *The Subtle Knife*, which are explored in Activity 8 (page 308).

2 As a class, return to the large circle. Using the space within the circle, Sculpt the characters of Will, Lyra, Pantalaimon and the boatman into the scene at this point in the play.

3 Discuss as a class the difficulties presented when taking the journey from script to stage. How would the director seeing the script for the first time know what is meant by 'Lyra and Pantalaimon feel the pain of separation' without having read and understood the novel? What does this say about the adaptation process? Is it the playwright or the director/actors who make the decisions about positioning, facial expressions and gestures? Does the playwright include many stage instructions?

4 A member of the class is given the role of the 'playwright' (Nicholas Wright).

   a Position the playwright in the frozen scene where you think he should be.

   b Justify your choice, using evidence from the text to support your ideas. Discuss the positioning as a class. Throughout the discussion, other students should demonstrate the position they feel is most appropriate by moving and Placing the playwright and justifying their choice.

   c Discuss whether this differs from the position of the writer placed earlier. Why?

   d A student representing the 'audience' can now be placed in the same way. A discussion can take place about the difference between Placing the Reader and Placing the Audience. Is there any? Discuss what this tells us about the adaptation process.

What have I learnt?

- How does physically Placing the Playwright and Audience help your understanding of the writer's perspective and techniques?
- How did this process develop your understanding of the adaptation process? What decisions do you feel the playwright had to make? Why?
- Are there aspects of the script that you would have done differently? Explain your comments by using evidence from the texts and by referring to the activities you have completed.

Activity 10: Does the writer remain? Does Philip Pullman have a role in the script?

Learning outcomes

You will:

- transfer your understanding of the adaptation process of *His Dark Materials* to think critically about the role of writers in other adaptations
- analyse the relationship between writer and scriptwriter and the differences/similarities between the role of the reader and that of the audience
- make decisions and select evidence to support your decisions and ideas.

You will do this by considering the role of the original writer in the adapted version of the play and questioning the significance of this to the general process of adaptation.

1 Return to the sculpted scene from the play described in Activity 9 (page 308), which includes the playwright and the audience.

  a The student who represented the writer (Philip Pullman) should stand at the side of the frozen scene. Should Philip Pullman, the writer, be placed into the scripted scene and, if so, where? Does the original writer remain part of the text? Are they left outside the scene? Are they near to the playwright or do they have a different perspective?

  b Position the writer where you feel it is most appropriate for them to be.

2 Discuss with the class whether they agree with your positioning. Throughout the discussion, other students should demonstrate the position they feel is most appropriate by moving and Placing the Writer and justifying their choices. Discuss what this might tell us about the adaptation process. Would this be the case with all adaptations?

3 Discussion can also take place about the sense of loss created in this scene. What aspects of your life or other students' lives can be related to the feelings in this scene?

4 The writer, playwright and audience and so on are stripped away from the scene to leave just the frozen sculpted characters of Lyra and Will. While the two characters remain frozen, read lines 1–34 from Part 2, Act two, Scene 12 (pages 266–267)

from	WILL	Just breathe.
to	JOPARI	Because for us, there's no elsewhere.

What have I learnt?

- How have the tasks in this activity helped your understanding of this particular scene and the adaptation process?
- What might the actors or director gain from taking part in similar activities?
- Who did you find most difficult to position? Why? What skills/understanding were required for this?

Activity 11: The final scene – Communal Voice to make a single decision

Learning outcomes

You will:

- explore the ending of the play
- analyse the significance of the two worlds and how the staging of both worlds at once can be achieved
- use your understanding gained from all the other activities to approach the ending of the play critically and with integrity
- demonstrate an understanding of the drama process.

You will do this by creating an oral script through the use of Communal Voice and re-enacting the end of the play.

1 Projected onto walls at opposite ends of the room are the two images of the Botanic Gardens, used at the beginning of the work. (Alternatively, your teacher may hand out photocopies of the images.)

2 Read lines 1–33 from Part 2, Act Two, Scene 15 (pages 276–277)

from	LYRA	Pan! Oh, Pan, you're back!
to	SERAFINA	. . . all that is good will die unless you stop it.

3 A member of the class is given the role of Serafina. She is sculpted by another student into the position they believe she will be in when the action takes place.

4 Other members of the class are given the roles of Lyra and Will. They are all sculpted into the scene and freeze while the teacher and two other students read lines 34–52:

from	LYRA	*How* is it flowing?
to	WILL	If I can't cut a window, then we . . .

5 The remaining members of the class are asked who they think would speak first and what they would say.

- **a** When you (or another student) suggest the next line to be spoken, the characters remain frozen, while you go to stand behind the character you will speak for.
- **b** The end of the extract is read again, after which you will speak the next line.
- **c** The remaining members of the class are then asked what they think the characters would say next. The individual students go and stand by the character who they think they can speak for.

6 The scene is frozen again after your teacher has explained that one by one the people behind the sculpted characters will continue the scene by speaking their thoughts or speech. Using **Communal Voice** continue the conversation between Lyra, Will and Serafina. What will they decide to do?

Communal Voice individual members of the group take up positions, one at a time, behind a sculpted character and speak the words that character says at a chosen moment in the drama.

7 The scene is frozen again. Your teacher hands out the lines from the play that Lyra and Will speak towards the end in the Botanic Gardens. The students who have been Will's voice are given Will's lines and the students who have provided Lyra's voice are given her lines. The students turn to face the projected pictures at either end of the room, or look at the photocopies handed out by your teacher. The sculpted characters of Lyra and Will remain frozen throughout in the centre of the room. Music may be played quietly in the background.

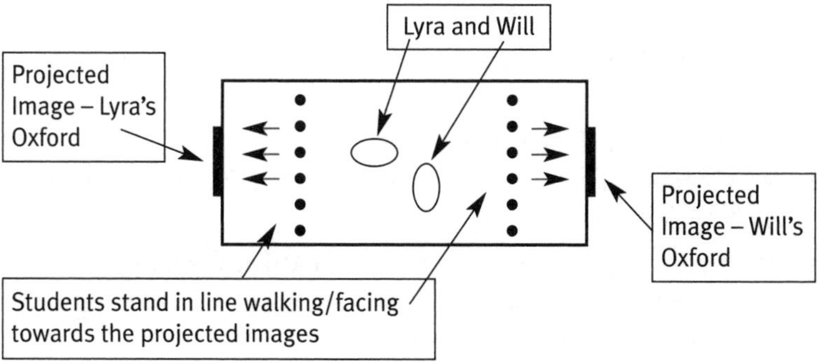

If you are looking at photocopies of the images handed out by your teacher, imagine instead that the images are on the wall.

8 The first student steps towards the picture (Lyra's Oxford) on the wall that they are facing.

a As they do so, say lines 90–93 from Part 2, Act Two, Scene 15 (pages 279–280)

LYRA I want to kiss you and lie down with you . . . until I die

b The first student on Will's side (with his back to Lyra's first student) steps towards the picture (Will's Oxford) they are facing and says lines 93–95 from page 279: 'I'll always love you. And when I die, I'll drift about forever, all my atoms, till they mix with yours.'

c The second student on Lyra's side then steps towards Lyra's Oxford and says line 96: 'Every atom of you, every atom of me.'

d The process continues until the final two students reach lines 113–114

LYRA Goodbye.

WILL Goodbye.

Everyone remains frozen for a few seconds and then music may be played.

What have I learnt?

- How have the final tasks in Activity 11 helped you to develop your understanding of the end of the play?
- What benefit might the actors or directors gain from taking part in such an activity?
- Think back to the Guided Tour activity in Activity 2a (page 285). What aspects of the two worlds have remained the same and what have changed? Why?
- How should the final 'goodbyes' be said? Why? Provide evidence to support your decision.

Reflecting on the activities

- Which skills have you developed or learnt through this work? How will your teacher be able to tell you have learnt or developed these skills?
- Which activity do you think helped you most to enjoy, understand and/or analyse the play? Why?
- Choose two other scenes from the play and think about which drama activities or conventions you could use to explore these scenes. Explain why you would use those particular activities and what you would be expecting people to learn from them.
- Choose two of the activities, either from those you have already done or that you have devised, that you feel a director about to stage the play should use with the actors. Explain your choice and justify why you think it would be of benefit to those involved in a performance of *His Dark Materials*.

Glossary

Action Narration a convention which requires each participant to pause and verbalise motives and descriptions of actions before they undertake them in improvisation

Action Reading you, and other students, in role, walk through a scene, speaking lines and adding gestures and movements, while reading from scripts

Communal Voice individual members of the group take up positions, one at a time, behind a sculpted character and speak the words that character says at a chosen moment in the drama; individual voices can speak more than once; a dialogue can be staged in this way with sculpted characters facing each other while their 'voices' take positions behind each of them and speak only the utterances of that character; your teacher may speak in role as one of the characters to introduce a new element or information or play devil's advocate

Digital Video Clip a short, repeatable dramatic sequence is 'bookended' with a Still Image at the start and a Still Image at the end

Describe/Name the Space participants are invited to offer words to describe a physical (or metaphorical) space between two characters at a moment of tension in the drama; the same technique can be used to describe barriers that exist between character or situations

Guided Tour in pairs, **A** (with eyes open) leads **B** (with eyes closed) slowly through an imaginary environment, providing a spoken commentary; the environment or location may be based on text but will usually be stimulated by a printed or projected map or picture

Placing the Author in order to help you to appreciate an author's perspective, you or your teacher represent the presence, at a defined moment in the drama, of the author; supposedly unseen by the actors (frozen at a significant moment), the author is sculpted into the scene by individual students who justify the positioning by drawing on evidence from the text; the act of placing the author is carried out as many times as demonstrates the range of possible author perspectives at any one moment in the drama

Placing the Audience/Reader a similar process to **Placing the Author** but here you or your teacher represent the presence and/or perspective of the audience or reader at a defined moment in the drama

Rolling Theatre a means by which groups can share their work on different aspects of a drama, learning from each other by running several rehearsed sections in a sequence; the theatrical integrity of the sequence will be the result of each group taking total responsibility for the start and finish of their section, independent of the need for teacher intervention; this may be achieved through the use of strong Still Images at the beginning and end of the Digital Video Clips signalling the contribution of the next group in a pre-arranged theatrical sequence

Role on the Wall this convention is used to help you define character traits at particular moments in a drama; sticky notes or cards with written statements or words are positioned on a large outline of a particular character usually pinned on a wall or laid on the floor. You may write your own words or statements or your teacher may write them. It is important that if you have contributed the word you are given the card or sticky note to place where you think appropriate on the outline (near the head or the heart for example)

Sculpting participants offer suggestions to place an individual in a significant, frozen position so that considered analysis can be made

Still Image/Still Picture/Freeze-Frame a still image is created by participants in the drama standing motionless, often at a given sign by your teacher or as a result of being sculpted by other students into the frozen image. This convention is used to mark a significant moment or enable time for reflection